Medieval Castles

Conrad Cairns

Published in cooperation with Cambridge University Press
Lerner Publications Company, Minneapolis

LIBRARY OF CONGRESS CATALOGING-IN-PUBLICATION DATA

Cairns, Conrad.
　　Medieval castles / Conrad Cairns.

　　　p.　　cm. — (A Cambridge topic book)
　　Reprint. Originally published: Cambridge [Cambridgeshire]:
Cambridge University Press, ©1987.
　　"Published in cooperation with Cambridge University Press."
　　Includes index.
　　Summary: A history and discussion of those fortified private
dwellings, known as castles, which were built in Europe only during
the Middle Ages, with particular attention to those of Britain.
　　ISBN 0-8225-1235-1 (lib. bdg.)
　　1. Civilization, Medieval — Juvenile literature. 2. Castles —
History — Juvenile literature. 3. Castles — Great Britain — History
— Juvenile literature. [1. Castles. 2. Castles. — Great Britain.
3. Civilization, Medieval.] I. Title.
[CB353.C34 1989]　　　　　　　　　　　　　　　　88-23648
940.1 — dc19　　　　　　　　　　　　　　　　　　　CIP
　　　　　　　　　　　　　　　　　　　　　　　　AC

This edition first published 1989 by Lerner Publications Company
by permission of Cambridge University Press.

Original edition copyright © 1987 by Cambridge University Press
as part of *The Cambridge Introduction to the History of Mankind: Topic Book*

International Standard Book Number: 0-8225-1235-1
Library of Congress Catalog Card Number: 88-23648

Manufactured in the United States of America

This edition available exclusively from:
Lerner Publications Company, 241 First Avenue North, Minneapolis, Minnesota 55401

1　2　3　4　5　6　7　8　9　10　98　97　96　95　94　93　92　91　90　89

Contents

1 **The earliest castles** *p.4*
Byzantines, Arabs, Spaniards *p.4*
The Frankish Empire fails *p.5*
Castles of earth and timber *p.7*

2 **Stone rather than wood** *p.10*
The square keep *p.10*
The shell keep *p.11*
The curtain wall *p.12*

3 **The castle under siege** *p.12*

4 **Improving the defences** *p.16*
Holding the land *p.16*
Lessons from the Crusades *p.16*
Stronger keeps *p.18*
Hitting the attackers *p.20*
Stronger curtain walls *p.22*
Guarding the gate *p.23*
Frederick, Wonder of the World, and his castles *p.29*

5 **Designing perfect castles** *p.30*
Concentrating the power *p.30*
The line of defence *p.31*
The North Wales castles of Edward I *p.34*

6 **The castle as a house to live in** *p.36*

7 **The smaller castles** *p.40*
The fortified manor house *p.40*
The 'four-square' castle *p.41*
The tower-house *p.42*

8 **The decline of the castle** *p.44*
Gunpowder *p.44*
The king's peace *p.46*
Stately homes and ancient monuments *p.47*

Glossary p.49
Index p.50
Acknowledgments p.52

A castle can be defined simply as a fortified private dwelling, designed to be secure against armed attack.

Most fortifications are not castles; for example, frontier defences, town walls or forts with garrisons of regular soldiers do not belong in this category. On the other hand, there are great houses with 'castle' in their names that are completely unfortified, built after the time of real castles. Genuine castles were built in Europe only during the Middle Ages. The earliest appeared at a time when people were living under the constant danger of violence. Afterwards castles were developed and improved to meet new challenges until at last they seemed perfect. But conditions went on changing, and eventually castles were no longer effective in war or convenient in peace. Then they were altered to become luxurious mansions, or left to fall into ruin.

But castles had been built to endure, and many of them still stand firm in countryside or town. Often we may look upon them as survivors from a more romantic age, when life was more adventurous, heroic and brutal. The people who lived in those castles, though, were probably neither more nor less brutal and heroic than people nowadays. To them a castle was a working building, sensible and practical.

This book is mainly about the castles that can be seen in Britain, but to understand them properly, we must know how castles first began and developed in other lands.

1　The earliest castles

The Romans were mighty builders, but they had no place for private strongholds like castles in their system of law and strict government. The Roman army knew that it was better, whenever possible, to move forward against an enemy, and not wait behind walls to be attacked. All the same, they knew that fortifications, properly used, could be very helpful, and they built a great variety throughout their empire, especially in the frontier provinces. But no defences against outside enemies could save a society from decaying within, and the Roman Empire in the West collapsed during the fifth century.

It was split up into many kingdoms, and the new rulers were barbarians, tribesmen from the Germanic lands. These people had always lived in wooden settlements, their chief in a large barn-like hall in their midst. Naturally, they liked this way of life better than Romanised ways. When they took over

Byzantine fort at Lemsa, Tunisia, as it may have looked about 650. The rectangular plan, simple but efficient, was to reappear often in castles of later centuries.

Roman provinces they often chose not to live in the towns, but in the country. Meanwhile, trade had been badly upset, and many towns became poor and ruined. This neglect of towns was most likely to happen in the northern lands, where the Angles, Saxons and Franks settled. Here a few towns may have kept their walls in repair, but generally very little was built in stone, neither fortifications nor anything else.

Byzantines, Arabs, Spaniards

It was different in the Mediterranean lands. Here the craft of building in stone continued, and the newcomers forgot their wooden halls and huts. Over the eastern Mediterranean, the Eastern Roman Empire still held sway, strong and vigorous— though its language was Greek rather than Latin and its capital was not Rome but Constantinople, or Byzantium, to use its original name.

Here there was no neglect of fortifications. The Byzantine Empire faced many enemies, and its military engineers were just as skilled as their Greek and Roman ancestors. They built and maintained huge, complex defences around the great cities, best of all the triple wall of Constantinople itself. They also developed comparatively small forts that could guard exposed or newly occupied territories. Their strategy was that in time of invasion or rebellion these forts could hold until reinforcements arrived. They were not castles; they were regular Byzantine army posts. But they looked very much like some of the castles that were to be built in later centuries and may have provided the idea for them.

In the seventh century the Arabs swept across the Middle East, conquering in the name of their new faith, Islam. They reached Constantinople but could not breach its mighty walls. Nevertheless, they became rulers of many rich provinces of the Byzantine Empire and quickly adopted the skills of their new subjects. Soon the Arabs were erecting splendid buildings.

The Muslims, as believers in Islam were called, spread westwards along the North African coast and reached the Straits of Gibraltar. In 711 they crossed and, within a few years, were masters of nearly all the Iberian peninsula. Southern Spain became one of the great centres of Islamic civilization, with its capital at Cordoba. In the north, however, there was a long strip of mountains where Christian Spaniards took refuge and would not submit, no matter how often the Muslims attacked and punished them. At first they did not seem very important, but gradually they grew stronger and started pushing southwards, trying to win back land from the Moors – their name for the Muslims. So began a struggle that lasted from the ninth century until the end of the Middle Ages, when in 1492 the last Moorish king surrendered Granada to the Christians.

During those centuries, across the wide plains of central Spain people could rarely forget the threat of war, and even in time of truce those near the frontier were never safe from raids. They needed strongholds to protect their own lands and to be bases for attacks on the enemy. Walled towns did the job very well, but there could not be enough of them to cover the long frontier. Therefore the Moors built smaller stone strongholds, something like the Byzantine forts they had encountered in North Africa, and the Christians soon copied. Kings granted special privileges to the citizens of walled towns in return for guarding the district. In the same way, they allowed warrior lords to hold the smaller fortresses as their own, on condition that they and their men protected the land and fought for their king when he needed them. So these were not

Moorish castle of Banos de le Encina, near Jaén in southern Spain, as it may have looked about 960. A high wall, made stronger by many towers, encircles the crest of a hill.

the forts of a regular army, they were the first castles in Europe. There were so many, both Moorish and Christian, that central Spain became known as *Castilla*, Castile or the land of castles.

The Frankish Empire fails

The Spanish castles were successful, but they were not copied; castles developed differently in northern Europe. This may have been because there was not much contact with Spain, but more probably because conditions in the north were so different. As we saw, wood was the natural building material there. Apart from repairs to some of the old Roman walls, stone was used only for building churches and, very rarely, palaces. It was still possible for wealthy people to hire stone-carvers and even architects – if necessary, from Italy – but stone was expensive, slow and cold.

Another difference was in methods of warfare. Northern warriors were always fighting, but usually against people like themselves, and they all shared a tradition that brave soldiers usually came out to do battle in the open. So, apart from town walls that had survived from Roman times, their strongholds were not elaborately fortified. An Anglo-Saxon *burh*, for instance, would probably have begun as a timber-built settlement protected by an earth bank and palisade, placed if possible on a site with natural advantages, such as on a hill or between streams.

The greatest of all northern warriors was Charles, King of the Franks (often called Charlemagne). After making himself ruler of most of north-west and central Europe he tried, in 800, to found something that would replace the old Roman Empire. It became known as the Holy Roman Empire. But Charles was trying to do it without the highly organised system of government that the Romans had used. His empire lacked the laws and law-courts, the magistrates and trained administrators, the network of communications and, above all, the regular army of the old empire. Instead, Charles had to rely on the loyalty of his nobles, warrior leaders like himself, to rule and protect their districts in his name. Only a very strong king could enforce his will upon such men, especially over so wide an area. Charles' successors could not. Soon his empire was split into three, and still the rulers of these smaller realms often failed to provide their subjects with peace and order.

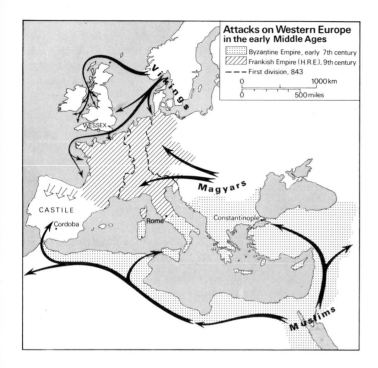

Attacks on Western Europe
in the early Middle Ages

- Byzantine Empire, early 7th century
- Frankish Empire (H.R.E.), 9th century
- --- First division, 843

0 — 1000 km
0 — 500 miles

especially awkward for the Magyars when they were making for home, probably tired and disorganised, burdened with loot and pursued by Henry's vengeful army.

Thus fortifications proved their value in northern Europe, but these were not castles.

Private strongholds seem to have developed because, in those dangerous decades, no lord was likely to survive for long unless his home could beat off an attack; and not only from Vikings or Magyars, but from greedy neighbours also. When the king was too weak to enforce law, lords must often have thought that they had no choice but to fortify their dwellings and hire good fighting men – at this time armoured horsemen were coming to be recognised as the most effective. So, in France and Germany, castles were appearing at about the same time as the medieval feudal system, and for the same reasons; in England it seems that nobles, though now they may have owned bigger and stronger halls, did not have the

West Saxon burh of Lydford, Devon, as it may have looked about 890. Protected by steep valleys on two sides, the palisaded earth ramparts were 40 feet (12 metres) thick.

While Charles' empire was falling apart, its peoples were becoming prey to increasingly devastating raids by two races of ruthless invaders, the Vikings and the Magyars. The Vikings in their ships and the Magyars on their horses would appear suddenly, loot, burn and kill, and be away before a big enough army could gather to beat them. Local forces and palisaded villages had no chance.

Fortification was one answer. A king might establish well-fortified towns in key positions and put trustworthy men in charge of them. In England, Alfred the Great, after repelling a Viking invasion of Wessex, covered the kingdom with a system of such burhs in the 880s. Early in the next century Henry the Fowler of Germany set up a similar system of strongholds, some of them walled in stone, to check the Magyars. Those wild raiders wanted quick loot, not time-consuming sieges for which they lacked equipment and experience. Their problem was not only that much of the best loot would now be behind those walls, but that now, if they plunged into Germany without taking the towns on their route, or at least leaving strong forces behind to blockade them, the garrisons would follow, harass and try to delay them; this would be desire – or perhaps the opportunity – to build castles.

To a king, castles could be either a hindrance or a help. Rebellious lords would be much harder to tame if they held castles, but in the hands of loyal lords castles could strengthen the kingdom. Kings often tried to insist that no house could be fortified without a royal licence, and strong kings destroyed castles that had been built without permission – adulterine castles, as they were called. Kings also tried to reserve for themselves, as their own property, the greatest castles in the most important positions.

Castles were useful not only in defending a well-established kingdom, but also in holding newly conquered lands. That was how castles came to England. In 1066 the Normans carried in their invasion fleet prefabricated wooden parts for a castle to protect their landing-place, and after their victory they planted castles all over England to check revolts and guard against new invaders. The Scots learned about castles from Normans invited as friends by their king, and the Welsh through fighting the Norman lords who seized land on the Marches. Finally, after invading Ireland in 1169, the Normans lost no time in placing castles in all the areas they occupied.

Castles of earth and timber

The vast majority of early Norman castles in Britain looked nothing like our usual picture of a castle. Instead of battlemented stone walls and lofty towers they were earthworks, embanked enclosures with, very often, a conical mound beside, topped by wooden walls, or *palisades*, strengthened by timber supports, or *revetments*, and containing wooden buildings. Today only the mounds and banks remain, weathered and overgrown; until early in this century, historians believed that they must have been made earlier, perhaps by Anglo-Saxons or Vikings, because they looked so unlike the massive stone cathedrals and keeps for which Norman builders were famed.

Yet these apparently primitive works fulfilled all that was required of a castle. They would include every building needed for a complete, self-contained community to carry on its daily life safely: lodgings for the guards, craftsmen, grooms, cooks, servants of all sorts, and their families; stores for food and equipment; stables and pens for the more valuable animals, especially the precious warhorses; workshops and kitchens; rooms for the lord, his family and guests; a chapel; and, most prominent in all this crowd of buildings, the hall. For the medieval barons, like the barbarian chieftains before them, the hall was the centre and the symbol of their power. Here all the important business of the castle and the district would be transacted (the local court, for instance) and here the castle people would assemble to dine. At meal-times the lord and his guests would sit on the dais, a low platform at one end of the hall, so as to see and be seen, while the rest sat at long trestle tables that could easily be removed when the meal was over and the hall was needed for something else.

These buildings were grouped within the enclosure, known as the *bailey*, surrounded by the earth bank and palisade. It was this defence that turned the household into a castle. Often the whole bailey would be on high ground, with a ditch crossed by a drawbridge.

Thus far, the castle may have appeared simply as a

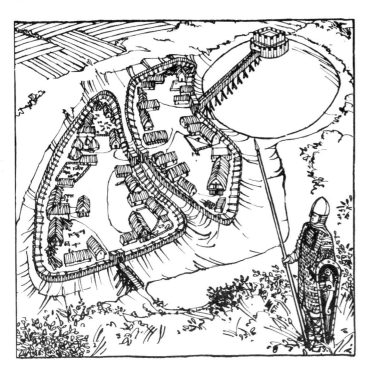

Norman castle at Brinklow, Warwickshire, as it may have looked about 1130. Probably the hall would have stood in the inner bailey, with barns, byres and sheds in the outer.

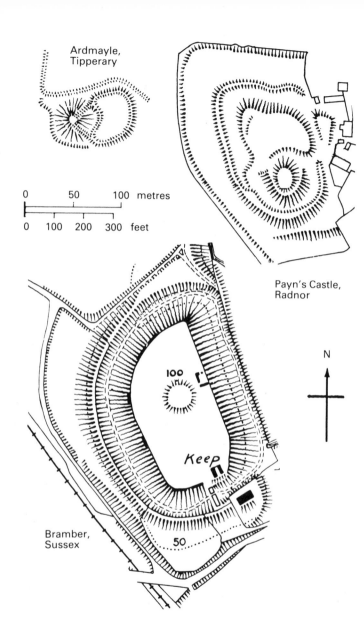

Ardmayle,
Tipperary

0   50   100 metres
0 100 200 300 feet

Payn's Castle,
Radnor

N

100

Keep

Bramber,
Sussex

50

Plans from Early Norman Castles of the British Isles *(1912), the book in which Mrs E. Armitage proved that these earth-works were Norman. Common in many areas, they vary in size and arrangement, but the simpler plans are the more usual. Recent scholars have pointed out numerous 'ringworks' with ditches but no motte; it is arguable whether or not these were strong enough to be properly called castles.*

strengthened version of an earlier type of settlement. Such fortifications are nowadays termed *ringworks*. When a castle had a *motte*, as so many of them did, the difference became obvious. The motte was the conical mound next to (occasionally within) the bailey. It was meant as a strong place of refuge. There usually was not much space on top, just enough for a palisade around the edge and a wooden tower in the middle. But if an enemy took the bailey, the lord and a few others could hold the motte until relief arrived, or they came to some arrangement with the enemy. Sometimes the lord and his supporters were able to escape under cover of darkness.

The wooden motte-and-bailey castle cost little and was efficient. It was quick and easy to construct, for the wood-cutting and digging needed no special skills beyond what any peasant or soldier would have. Its high banks could prove very difficult to storm, and even royal armies had trouble in subduing a castle of this type. Palisade defences, indeed, have always been acknowledged as useful; as recently as the 1960s, they were employed in Vietnam.

Their defects, though, were serious. Wood that is in constant contact with the ground soaks up water and tends to rot, so palisades needed regular attention. There was a limit on size, for it is difficult to erect strong high walls of wood. Sometimes the tower on the motte must have been too cramped for its garrison, and sometimes the outer defences must have been low enough for a numerous and determined enemy to scramble over. But probably the worst fault of all was that wood burned. The famous Bayeux Tapestry shows Normans forcing a castle to surrender by putting fire-brands to it.

In many parts of Europe, wooden castles were never popular. As we have seen, in the south, where skills of building in stone had never been lost, there was no need to resort to wood; besides, good building wood was not as plentiful as in the north, and in hot summers wood becomes an even greater fire risk. In northern Europe the Germans themselves, despite their old liking for wood, preferred to put their castles on rocky hilltops, where building stone was near and where it would have been absurd to chisel holes in the rock merely to set in the timbers of palisades.

The truth seems to be that the earth-and-wood castle was always recognised as being a cheap or temporary stronghold, and even where it was common—in Britain and northern France—it soon gave place to stone.

Some early types of stone defences in north-west Europe

left: *The famed monastery of Kells as it may have looked about 1100. In fear of Viking and other raiders, Irish monks began after 800 to build tall, thin towers beside their clusters of 'bee-hive' huts. Here they were safe, but could not fight back nor remain for long; the hope was that raiders would loot the huts and move on.*

below left: *Near the Rhine, German castle-builders found crags that were natural strongholds, where they could safely erect comfortable dwellings. On the summit they usually built a tower of refuge or* bergfried *(literally translated, 'mountain peace'), much better designed for defence than the Irish towers. This view of St Ulrichsburg, Alsace, shows the strength of the position and the tower, with the palatial buildings added below in the twelfth century.*

below: *In Western Scotland, too, stone was a natural building material. Castle Sween, Argyll, is simply a strong wall, without towers but with battlements originally; living quarters were built against the inner face of the wall. It dates from around 1100, and several similar castles were built on rocky sites along the west coast, while Norman-style earth castles were appearing in other parts of Scotland.*

2 Stone rather than wood

Though the motte-and-bailey remained the most common sort of castle in England and northern France until well into the twelfth century, kings and great lords who could afford the expense had been building stone castles for a long time. Not only were these stronger, but they made the owner appear grander. The stone castles had the same basic plan as the wooden ones—a defended courtyard plus a strongpoint—but this plan was carried out in two different ways.

The square keep

In 994 Fulk Nerra (the Black), Count of Anjou in central France, built a two-storeyed, thick-walled tower at Langeais. Its shape was something like a high stone version of a wooden hall, and perhaps that is just what the builders had in mind.

Colchester, the largest keep in Britain, was built about 1080 on the ruins of a Roman temple. Its walls are 17½ feet (5.3 m) thick at the base, and its original height is shown in line.

Langeais was one of the earliest of the so-called square keeps; in fact most were not square, but rectangular, and *keep* is a modern term for what used to be called a *donjon*. Those that remain are an impressive sight today, and they certainly impressed people then. For about two hundred years, square keeps were the strongest class of fortification in France and Britain; the Normans were particularly fond of them and built them wherever they went, from Ireland to Sicily.

The most famous of all British castles, the Tower of London, was begun by William I soon after the Norman Conquest, and his keep, the White Tower, looks today much as he left it. There was a tendency for the shape of keeps to change, becoming higher in proportion to their width. Rochester keep, built in 1126, is one of the best examples in England of a big twelfth-century square keep (page 15).

Inside one of these keeps, the lord could live comfortably all the time. The main room was the great hall, which would usually occupy the whole of one of the upper floors, sometimes rising to the roof of the keep and with a gallery all around, high up, in the thickness of the wall. The entrance to the keep would normally be on the second floor, approached by an outside flight of stairs; that floor would probably have the guard-room and store-rooms. There would be more stores of food, drink and munitions in the basement or first floor, and, if possible, a well. The lord and his guests would probably have the luxury of private bed-chambers built in the thickness of the keep wall, and by the twelfth century the finest of these might even have fireplaces. Lesser folk would have to make up their beds in one of the main rooms, perhaps near to where they worked. Also built into the thickness of the walls there would be several small chambers which are often called *garderobes*. Perhaps people sometimes did hang clothes there—it was said that moths did not like the atmosphere—but the main purpose of these rooms was as latrines. Sanitation was especially important where many people might be crowded together in a siege, and most castle-builders seem to have been well aware of this.

Still, many lords preferred to live most of the time in a great hall in the bailey, because the keep was, after all, built more for strength than comfort. The walls were immensely thick, often ten feet (three metres) or more, to resist battering rams or stones hurled by siege engines. There were few, if any, windows on the lower floors, and even higher up they were often

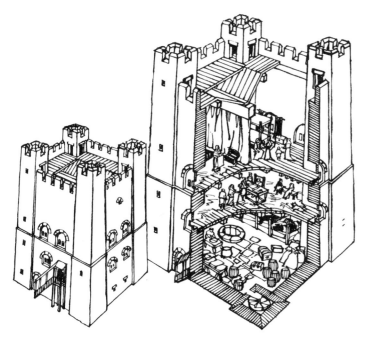

Appleby keep, Cumbria, as it may have looked about 1180. With walls only 6 feet (1.8 metres) thick, no forebuilding and a door direct into the cellar, it was more house than fortress.

The shell keep

No doubt every lord would have liked to build his castle with a square stone keep. But the expense of such a quantity of stone and the skilled workmen to build the keep could be too much, especially when a lord was establishing himself. There was also the problem of the foundations. A square keep was tremendously heavy. A lord who wanted to replace the wooden defences of his motte-and-bailey with stone would have to think carefully; his motte probably would not be firm enough, especially an artificial motte. Of course he might build his keep somewhere else; the middle of the bailey was a common location. But there was a way of keeping the motte in use.

This was simply to put a stone wall around the edge of the motte, in place of the palisade. Such a wall is known as a *shell*. Normally it would be circular, but it could follow the irregular outline of a natural motte. There would be a gateway through the shell, often guarded by a tower; occasionally the builders would construct a covered causeway to protect people climbing to the gate against the missiles of attackers.

Inside the shell, built against it, would be the hall and other apartments, often of wood. They must have been cramped and

better placed for safety than admitting light. The keep was so high that it was very unlikely that an attacker could scale the battlements, whether by ladder or *belfry* (page 14), so builders put every sort of obstacle in the way of anybody trying to force an entry lower down. The outside stairs were usually covered by a defensive work called a *forebuilding*, and sometimes so arranged that the attackers had their right sides towards the defenders—for they carried their shields on their left. If attackers managed to batter their way through several stout doors into the keep, there were more obstacles. Many keeps were divided in two by a strong cross-wall, pierced by only one door on each floor. And the only way from floor to floor would be a narrow spiral staircase that could easily be blocked. Often the spiral would be arranged so that a right-handed man, standing above, could easily use his sword while his body was protected by the central newel of the stair, but the attacker, below, could only strike awkwardly and had no protection. A lord might be glad of such devices in times of trouble, even if they were not convenient in times of peace.

Trematon castle, Cornwall, shows clearly as a motte-and-bailey castle with shell keep and curtain walls. The square tower is a gatehouse added about 1250, and the house in the bailey was built in 1807, when a ruined castle was regarded as a fine picturesque setting for a gentleman's residence. Originally the lord's living quarters would have been built against the inside of the shell wall.

gloomy, with the shell walls blocking most of the sunlight, so it would not be surprising if people usually preferred to live in the bailey except in times of danger. In a few castles, there were, in fact, no buildings within the shell except for a small tower in the centre, a kind of inner keep that was made of either stone or wood.

The curtain wall

With keeps of either type, the bailey remained the centre of everyday life. Naturally, when he could afford it, the lord of a castle preferred a wall around his bailey to a palisade; stone would not rot, would not burn, and could be built higher. Such a wall around a castle bailey is known as a *curtain wall*.

So, by the middle of the twelfth century, all the up-to-date, good-quality castles in England and France were stone-built, with square or shell keeps and walled baileys. But the earth-and-wood castles still had many more years of usefulness, because they were so cheap and easy to build and repair. As we saw, the Anglo-Norman invaders of Ireland in 1169 used the timber castle in their first assault; it was so effective against the Irish, who had no experience of siege warfare, that twenty years elapsed before they bothered to build a stone castle. In York, the chief city of northern England, where there were two mottes, it was the late thirteenth century before a shell keep replaced the wooden defences on top of one, and the other motte went out of use before it could get a shell.

Meanwhile it became increasingly obvious that there was still a great deal to be done to improve stone castles before they could be considered really strong against a skilful attack. Before we consider those improvements, we need to see how such an attack might be conducted.

3   The castle under siege

Sometimes an attacker was able to capture a castle by surprise or because a traitor inside helped him. But in most cases he had to try to overcome the castle by a siege, and this would mean building machines to batter down walls or to help his men over them.

Long before gunpowder, there were other forms of artillery that flung rocks, fireballs, dead animals (to spread disease) and arrows at a fortress and its garrison. The pictures opposite show the two best-known types of siege engines in the Middle Ages. The *mangonel* had been known since ancient times—Roman soldiers called it 'the wild ass' because of its kick—but the more powerful and massive *trebuchet* first appeared in Europe during the twelfth century, though the Chinese and the Muslims had used similar weapons long before.

Engines could be made in many sizes, according to what was required. Besides battering walls or using engines similar to huge crossbows to clear defenders from the battlements, there was a need to put out of action the castle's own artillery. A castle might be equipped with the same sort of engines as the attackers, and though there was a limit to the size of what could be mounted on top of a tower, the extra height gave an important advantage. Also, the defenders would be practised in shooting from these positions, would know the range and just how well their engines could perform. A good example of defensive artillery positions can be seen at Harlech (page 35). The castle was designed to be supplied by sea, and platforms were sited from which engines could hit anyone trying to prevent ships from reaching the harbor.

The besiegers' engines might damage some of the defences, but it would take a long time to make much impression on the solid masonry of the strongest walls, and especially the keep. In some places the attackers might be able to deliver heavier blows more accurately with a battering ram or pry out stones one by one with picks and levers. This was dangerous work when the defenders were active above, so the attackers would have to take shelter under a *cat* or *penthouse*. These

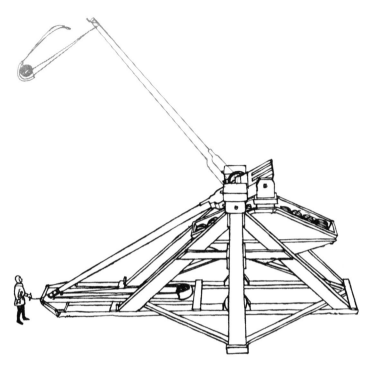

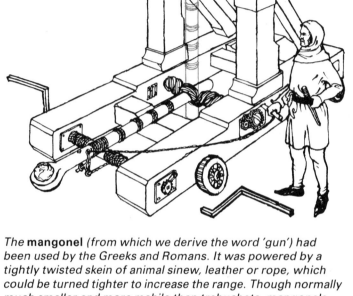

The **trebuchet** *was apparently the best-known missile engine. It worked on the see-saw principle: the greater the weight in the box on the short arm, the greater the force of the long throwing arm. Range could also be adjusted by changing the angle of the sling release prong at the end of that arm. With a high trajectory, trebuchets could drop missiles behind walls and hit the tops of towers. They could be built very large, but would then be difficult to move. This drawing is based on a one-twelfth scale working model.*

The **mangonel** *(from which we derive the word 'gun') had been used by the Greeks and Romans. It was powered by a tightly twisted skein of animal sinew, leather or rope, which could be turned tighter to increase the range. Though normally much smaller and more mobile than trebuchets, mangonels struck hard and, when fitted with a 'spoon' rather than a sling, more directly. This drawing is based on a full-scale reconstruction which could hurl a 10 lb (4.5 kg) stone accurately up to 350 yards (320 metres).*

were sturdy movable wooden sheds, covered with wet hides to make it harder for the defenders to set them on fire.

The most effective way to demolish part of a castle was, without doubt, the mine. From a concealed entrance somewhere in the besiegers' camp the miners would tunnel through the earth until they thought they were under the part of the castle they wished to bring down. There they would dig a large chamber, the roof held by wooden props. When the props were set on fire the chamber would fall in, and the stonework above would tumble into a heap over which a storming force could scramble.

Mining was a very risky and unpleasant job. The miner had to work in the dark, with little air, always in fear that the tunnel might fall in on him. Professional miners were valued and respected, for mining usually succeeded. A castle built on solid rock or surrounded by a deep moat or wet ground was safe against mining, but otherwise the only defence was to dig a countermine, so that the defenders could break into the besiegers' tunnel and kill the miners. To do this the defenders first had to find out where the mine was; they must keep a keen watch for suspicious movements outside the walls that might give away the position of a mine entrance, and then place bowls of water on the ground in likely places, hoping that the vibrations caused by the miners' picks in the earth would be enough to produce ripples on the water and show them where the mine was.

If a castle refused all demands to surrender, then sooner or later the attackers would have to take it by hand-to-hand combat. Unless they had battered down a gate or made a wide enough breach in the walls, they would have to *escalade* (scale or climb) the wall.

Scaling ladders were quick and easy to make and move, and so were popular for surprise assaults; but in other circumstances they were very dangerous, because the scalers could not shield themselves while clambering up the ladders, and the defenders could push the ladders with long poles and send them crashing away from the wall. When there was no chance of surprise it might be better to use a *belfry* or siege tower. This was a wooden tower, built higher than the wall it was to attack, on rollers so that it could be pushed up to the wall. Then a drawbridge at the top would be lowered onto the wall, attackers would rush across from the belfry and drive the defenders from the battlements. Sometimes, instead, the besiegers would build a stationary belfry – or even a 'siege castle' – some distance from the wall, high enough for archers to sweep the battlements clear of defenders so that scaling ladders could be used.

Once a belfry reached a castle wall it was fairly certain that the attackers would be able to overwhelm the defenders at that point and gain that part of the defences. But many a belfry would never get so far. The ground over which it must slowly be trundled had to be flat. When the defenders saw the besiegers filling in ditches and levelling hummocks they knew what to expect. The belfry's bulk and snail's pace made it a very easy target for every archer and engine that still survived within range. They might smash some of its beams, send it lurching over, and set it on fire despite its covering of wet hides. Because of these defects it seems that after the twelfth century belfries were used less, and attackers relied more on powerful pieces of artillery.

The defenders often had many advantages over the attackers – depending, of course, on how cleverly planned and strongly built their castle was. While the besiegers tried to shelter behind wooden screens, the defenders had stone battlements and, from the twelfth century, well-designed arrow-slits which

gave very good concealment and protection. Besides their engines and ordinary bows, they could use very powerful crossbows, slow to wind but easy to aim, that sent short, heavy, armour-piercing bolts with terrific force. (The English king Richard Lion Heart was mortally wounded in this way while besieging a castle.) In using all their weapons the garrison had the advantage of height, and this also allowed them to throw down rocks or scalding liquid on attackers; to lower huge pads to protect a stretch of wall being battered by stones or a ram; or to thrust downwards big wooden forks to catch the head of the ram. Finally, they could choose their time to attack their attackers. A party of them might sally forth at night, from a small door known as a *postern* or *sallyport*; with luck, they might catch the besiegers off guard, burn engines and kill workmen and get back to the castle while the camp was still waking up in confusion.

It is not difficult to understand why sieges could take a long time, and why soldiers loathed them. The attacking commander would need many more soldiers than there were in the castle, and would have the problem of preventing them from drifting away as the siege dragged tediously on; it was boring even more than it was dangerous and uncomfortable. If he thought he could not force his way in, the attacker might try to starve the garrison out; but in that case he would have the very difficult task of gathering enough supplies for his own men while they waited, more bored than ever. As time went on the risk grew that he might have to raise the siege because of hunger and discontent among his own men, or the approach of a relieving army.

If the siege ended in the castle being stormed, the garrison might be slaughtered. Attackers who had suffered hardship for weeks or months, and heavy loss as they fought their way in, would be in no mood to spare the people who had done this to them. Every soldier understood.

Neither side wanted to be killed if they could avoid it, and the besiegers would prefer to capture a castle in reasonable condition. Therefore it was quite common for the defenders, if they saw little hope of being relieved, to agree to surrender after, say, a week unless a relieving force arrived, and while waiting both sides would cease fighting. But however it ended, a siege cost the attacker time; the stronger the castle, the longer the time before surrender, and the better its chances of not having to surrender at all.

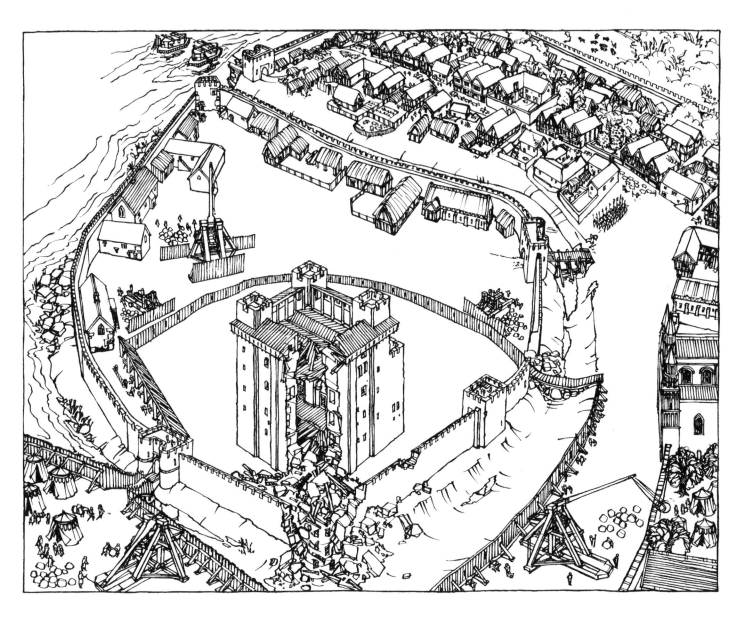

The last stage of the siege of Rochester castle, November 1215. Since early October King John's army, based comfortably in the town, had tightened its grip, cut the bridge to prevent relief, set up five great engines, broken into the bailey, undermined and brought down a corner of the huge keep. Even then the rebel barons held out behind the cross-wall that ran the whole height of the keep. The enraged king had sworn to kill them all, but eventually his advisers persuaded him to let them surrender safely. Some details of the scene have to be guessed, but we can be sure of others. There is no doubt, for example, about the damage to the keep; when it was repaired, about ten years later, the new corner turret was built in more up-to-date style – round – and the keep stands thus today.

4 Improving the defences

Holding the land

Medieval warriors and rulers—and no ruler was likely to prosper if he was a poor leader in war—knew very well the advantages that castles could give them. A relatively small force in a strong castle could hold off a much bigger force for weeks or months, and no prudent general would want to advance into enemy territory, leaving untaken a major castle whose garrison could threaten him from the rear. It is not surprising that campaigns sometimes revolved around castles, with sieges more common than pitched battles.

We have seen how the Normans used castles to hold newly conquered lands (page 7), and shall see Edward I of England using castles in the same way in Wales (page 34). They could be just as effective in preventing a country from being conquered, if they were properly located and held by reliable commanders. Richard Lion Heart built a superb castle, Chateau Gaillard (page 32), to block any French invasion of Normandy. But in 1204, only six years after Richard completed it, Chateau Gaillard was taken by King Philip Augustus of France, after a long and brave defence. The new king of England, John, had failed to do anything to stop Philip's army, and even the finest fortress must eventually fall if a powerful and determined enemy is allowed to attack it for long enough. But in 1216, Dover castle was held for King John by its constable, Hubert de Burgh, against an invading French army; he refused to surrender even after John died, and at last the French had to retreat.

Because they were proving so important, kings took great care about the main castles in their kingdoms, especially in areas where invasion was likely. They kept the key castles for themselves, under dependable constables, or allowed them to be held by a few lords whom they could watch closely. Near the Scottish border, for example, the Bishop of Durham had great powers and privileges, but he would need the king's help to resist a major Scottish invasion; besides, as a priest, he

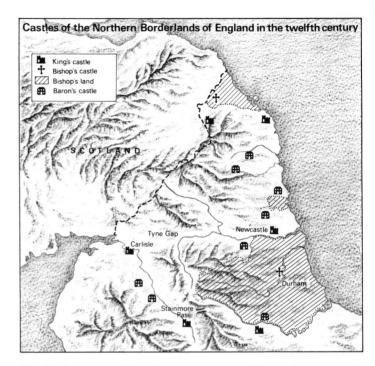

The fertile lowland, the river crossings and the main east–west routes were well guarded, with the king's and bishop's castles in the key positions. The system worked well; Scots invasions were usually disasters, sometimes with the king killed or captured. After about 1300 small raids increased, and many small castles were built to shelter the owners' people and cattle. This did not alter the strategic pattern.

could not leave heirs to inherit his position. When a bishop died, the king had the decisive word in 'electing' the new one.

Kings and lords soon realised that the keep-and-curtain castle was far from perfect. From about the middle of the twelfth century, they and their builders were constantly trying to improve their existing castles or this type, or experimenting with fresh designs.

Lessons from the Crusades

Historians used to suggest that most of the ideas for improving castles were brought by Crusaders returning from the Holy Land, where they had learned from Byzantine and Muslim fortifications how to plan castles more scientifically. It is true that the Crusaders did build magnificent castles. They needed them, especially during the later part of their occupation of Palestine, when they were usually desperately short of fighting men to meet attacks from the far more numerous Muslims. At first the Crusaders had not been so short of men, and their castles were simple keep-and-curtain affairs; but the later castles incorporated so many improvements, both in details and in overall design, that in the late twelfth century they were easily the strongest in the world.

Most of the devices described in this chapter and the next seem to have been used around the eastern Mediterranean before they appeared in Europe. But there is no definite proof that it was a case of straight copying, for European builders could have invented and adapted to suit the needs of whatever castle they were building. Every site had its own advantages and problems, and even if the architect had heard about the ideas used in the latest Crusader castles, he had to decide whether or how they could be fitted into his plans.

One new feature that was undoubtedly Crusader was the castle-monastery. This was copied from the *ribat*, a type of stronghold which the Muslims built on their frontiers against unbelievers; here devout believers volunteered to form the garrison and wage unceasing war against God's enemies, thus gaining the blessing of God as well as considerable booty. On the Christian side the Knights Templars and Hospitallers built the finest castles in the Holy Land, and the idea spread to other frontiers of Christian Europe where other military religious orders carried on the fight: in Castile, where the Knights of Alcantara, Calatrava and Santiago faced the Moors, and in Prussia where the Teutonic Knights were conquering, converting and ruling over the pagan tribes. But these establishments were a special feature of such frontiers, not found elsewhere. Besides, the castles were sometimes designed as much to be monasteries or centres of government as fortresses. They were certainly no more advanced than the castles that kings and great lords were building in other parts of Europe.

Crusader castles in contrasting lands. Margat (above) was a base of the Knights Hospitallers in the Holy Land. Despite its mountainous site, its size, its double ring of walls and great round keep at the 'sharp end', it finally surrendered to the Muslims in 1285. Marienburg (left) was the headquarters of the Teutonic Knights in West Prussia. Their castles were often brick-built (there was little good local stone) and arranged in high blocks around a square, part monasteries, part government offices. Marienburg was destroyed in the Second World War.

17

Stronger keeps

There are two main forms of defence, *passive* and *active*. The passive way is to absorb blows without suffering serious damage. The active way is to strike the attacker so that his blows are weakened. Castle designers used both principles, and we shall look first at the way they tried to improve the passive strength of castles.

The most important place to strengthen was obviously the castle's ultimate strongpoint, the keep. Its walls could be given reinforcing layers in the form of flat or *pilaster* buttresses. These undoubtedly made the walls more solid, but as props – the main purpose of buttresses – they were of little value. A good buttress must lean hard against its wall, and to do this it must stick out a good way; but even if the keep-builders fully understood this, they would not have wanted to provide such projections, which the enemy could either knock down fairly easily or use as cover in an assault.

A much more effective thickening was at the base, and here the stonework was often sloped outwards to form such a mass

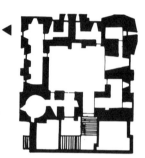

Third floor

Second floor

Two of Henry II's keeps. After the disorder of Stephen's reign, Henry destroyed many unlicensed baronial castles and built or strengthened royal castles at key places. Newcastle upon Tyne (left) shows the final development of the square keep: mighty walls with flat pilaster buttresses, corner turrets and strong plinth. The entrance is on the third floor, higher than usual, and covered by two turrets instead of a forebuilding. The battlements shown in this nineteenth-century print are recent restorations, almost certainly wrong. It was built by Maurice the Engineer in the early 1170s; he later built the keep at another strategic castle, Dover. Orford (right) was built in the late 1160s to watch the Suffolk coast and some untrustworthy local barons. It has, as shown in this eighteenth-century print, a more experimental design. Circular within and many-angled outside, with three large turrets, it has a normal forebuilding, second-floor entrance and big plinth.

18

At La Roche Guyon, also built in the late 1100s, the keep is circular, surrounded by a close protective wall or chemise which itself is partially enclosed by a lower wall. All have 'prows' or 'spurs' facing the expected direction of attack. Residential buildings are below, beside the river Seine.

stones would usually glance off its surface unless an engine hurled them very accurately indeed. There were many experiments with keeps built to such plans. Orford and Conisbrough combined them with big turrets and buttresses, which may have strengthened them in one way, but actually provided more angles for miners to attack. There were keeps in France built with a variety of rounded projections or lobes. But experience showed that simple circular towers gave the best results. Round towers had been built long before, in various countries and for various purposes; from the late twelfth century they became popular in French and British castles.

Despite all this, there are comparatively few circular keeps in Britain. Why? One reason was that so many square keeps already existed, and it would have been very expensive to pull down one of these merely to replace it with a round keep. Besides, a cylinder is less convenient for living in, and less economical than a rectangular building; it has less room than a square tower occupying a similar base and with equally thick walls. It might also be harder to build, with curved blocks of stone to be carefully shaped. So it was mainly on the Welsh Marches or in Wales, where Anglo-Norman lords were building castles that needed every device to withstand the fury of the people they were invading, that such great cylindrical towers were built.

of masonry that any attempt to smash through it would be futile. Such a feature is known as a *plinth*. An added advantage was that if a large body of attackers came close, stones dropped from the top of the tower would ricochet off the plinth into them, perhaps even splintering into sharp fragments. The plinth proved such an excellent device that it was used very widely – and there was no reason why a good idea should be used only on the keep. One variation on the plinth was a huge *spur* built out from a tower in the direction where attack was most likely; some French spurs are almost as big as the towers they are strengthening.

There was a fault of square keeps, however, that no amount of reinforcement could really correct – their right-angled corners. The sharper the angle of a tower, the more vulnerable it was to mining, and the easier to pick stones away. The only remedy was to build towers that did not have sharp corners. An octagonal tower could have corners only half as sharp. A round tower would have no corners at all, and

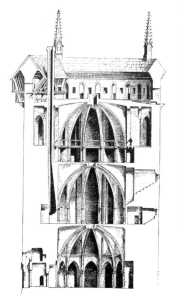

The keep at Coucy, north-eastern France. This nineteenth-century sectional drawing shows it as it probably was when built, about 1230–40. Note the stone vaults with central holes for light, the fine fireplaces and chimneys, the permanent hoarding with tiled roof. It also had its own moat. It was probably the most splendid round keep ever built, three times the area of Britain's biggest (Pembroke, page 26). It was destroyed in the First World War.

Hitting the attackers

Passive strength by itself was not enough. Without people to defend it even the strongest castle is helpless, and the castle-builder's job was to make it as easy and safe as possible for the defenders to be active. We saw in the last chapter how they were able to fight the besiegers from positions of strength, and now we shall see exactly what those positions were.

Shooting with a bow and arrow at somebody directly below is virtually impossible. An archer, therefore, could not hurt besiegers who were attacking the tower or wall on which he was standing. But if the archer were on, or in, a tower that projected from the wall, he could shoot along the face of the wall at the men attacking it. This made it safer and easier to aim; and, since the enemy would probably be crowded side by side, an arrow that missed one man might hit the next. Shooting along the enemy line from the side instead of straight at it from the front is known as *enfilading*. It was not a new idea, but as bows and engines were steadily being improved it became steadily more profitable to design castles to make full use of them.

There was usually no special problem in adding projecting towers to straight walls, though where a wall was curved or angled outwards the builder had to ensure that every part could be covered from at least one tower. Placing a tower on a corner, where its archers could sweep both sides of the angle, became usual. The extra strength that such towers provided led castle-builders to put a great deal more emphasis on the curtain wall, and we shall discuss their new ideas in the next section of this chapter.

Providing flanking or enfilading positions in a keep was less easy. Many keeps already had projecting turrets at the corners, but they usually did not stick out far enough to be useful for this purpose – they had been meant only to strengthen the corners of the building and to contain spiral stairs. The best solution was to build turrets that did not reach the ground, but were *corbelled* (built out) from the keep wall near the top. These corner-turrets became particularly popular in Spain, Ireland and Scotland – countries where square keeps and, later, tower-houses continued to be built all through the Middle Ages.

Despite all the emphasis on shooting, it was still very desirable to be able to drop stones or boiling liquid on attackers directly below. Battlements, especially the later forms, gave

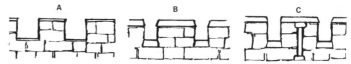

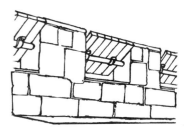

Battlements: *wide* crenels (gaps) *gave freedom to use arms* (A), *but as archery improved they tended to be made narrower* (B), *in extreme cases becoming mere slits while full arrow-slits were pierced in the* enlarged uprights *or* merlons (C). Crenels could have wooden shutters pivoted on iron bars (view from inside, right). Capstones on top of the merlons prevented rain from soaking and weakening the wall; they might also be shaped to deflect arrows.

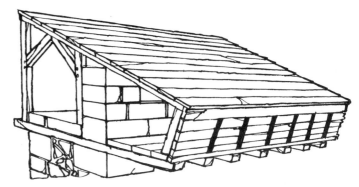

Hoardings: *covered galleries fitted outside the battlements gave extra concealment and protection, but were only wooden and must have been expensive to install. Many castles have square holes beneath their battlements for beams to support hoardings, though they may never actually have been fitted.*

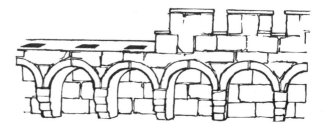

Machicolations: *strongly built as part of the wall itself, these projecting battlements were the best. They became increasingly common in the later Middle Ages.*

good protection to archers. But a defender had to lean out in order to drop a stone, and no *merlon* (upright) could protect him then from the besiegers' arrows; besides, some of the later *crenels* (gaps), designed only for shooting, were barely wide enough for leaning out and dropping things. The problem was solved by building strong wooden galleries outside the battlements, where defenders could move unseen by the besiegers and drop their loads through trapdoors in the floor. Such galleries were called *brattices* or *hoardings*. A few were permanent and have survived on continental castles. In Britain we can often see, just beneath castle battlements, a series of large square holes that were made to take the beams on which hoardings could be erected; in a few places long stones stick out of the wall instead.

Hoardings were very useful, but they had the disadvantages of wood; rocks and arrows might smash them or set them on

The shape of a tower affected the area of 'dead ground' in front which could not be covered by archers on the adjoining curtain wall.

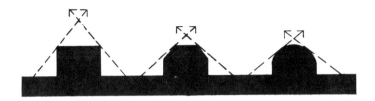

fire. So, as a stronger alternative, castle-builders corbelled the battlements themselves out from the walls, leaving gaps between the corbels through which the defenders could drop whatever they wished. This device was called *machicolation*. Like the use of flanking towers, it had been known to the Romans, but now it was revived and became very popular, especially for places that seemed most exposed to attack. Over doorways machicolations might be additionally useful for pouring water, if the attackers tried to burn down the door.

Arrowslits

had to be narrow outside   *roomy inside*   *with a wide angle for shooting.*

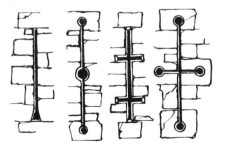

Many variations could be introduced:

fishtails allowed better shooting downwards, crosses and circles gave more light and a better view.

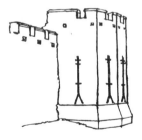

At Warkworth the Grey Mare's Tail tower has multi-storey slits more than 17 feet (5 metres) long. (Note also the shape, plinth, and holes for hoarding beams.)

At Caernarvon some slits were designed to be used by three archers at the same time, and in other places one archer had three slits.

Stronger curtain walls

The improvements we have been considering in relation to keeps could, of course, be just as valuable on other parts of the castle – sometimes more so. In applying the idea of enfilading to the curtain wall (page 20) the builders saw the possibility of making the defences of the bailey so strong that the defenders would rarely be forced to retreat to the keep.

The curtain wall towers would be spaced within easy bow-shot, so as to protect one another. Each would be made strong enough to hold out independently, in case other towers or stretches of wall should be taken by the enemy. Thus an attacker would find that a success in one place did not give him the whole outer part of the castle. The door from the curtain wall-walk into a tower was always small and strongly barred; sometimes there was no door at this level, and the only way into the tower was from the bailey. A tower would be of whatever size and shape best suited the defensive scheme of the particular castle. It was quite common to make the side facing the attacker round or many-angled, while the side within the bailey was flat. Sometimes an especially important wall-tower might almost be a second keep.

Making the towers independent of the wall was an idea carried even further by some Spanish castle-builders. They placed their towers outside the walls, connecting with the battlements only by a flying bridge. Such a tower was called a *torre albarrana*, and its archers could shoot soldiers attacking the main wall not only from the side, but from the rear. It was a daring scheme. The towers stood out in what seemed a perilously isolated position. In reality they were much less exposed than they appeared, but still the idea did not appeal to castle-builders in other countries. In France and Britain the rare examples of towers built outside the walls are very big and strong, keeps in fact, as at Coucy and Flint.

An even more daring idea was to disregard the use of towers as strongpoints capable of standing alone, and treat them as merely parts of one continuous line of defence that must be preserved unbroken. The disadvantage of a strong wall-tower was that if attackers managed to get inside it, they could use it against the castle garrison. Some builders, therefore, used half-towers. These were just like towers on the outside of the castle, but had no backs. If attackers got into one of these they would find no protection. Very probably they would not even find a place to stand, as the floors were sometimes no more

22

At Flint (plan, page 34) the circular keep acts as corner tower to the inner bailey and dominates the weak outer, but is also an independent stronghold with its own moat. The idea may have been copied from Coucy (page 19) or the Spanish *torres albarranas, or even from the old mottes, which normally stood outside their baileys.*

Framlingham, Suffolk, begun before 1200, relies entirely on its curtain wall; the towers are open at the back, so as to give no protection to an enemy who got inside. But such a scheme depends on the defenders having a central keep from which to shoot. We have no evidence why one was not built, nor even whether plans were made for one.

than movable platforms which the defenders of the castle had had time to draw back. Framlingham, begun about 1180, probably by Roger Bigod, Earl of Norfolk, appears to have relied wholly on its curtain wall, with no strongpoint or inner defence where the defenders could rally if the curtain should be penetrated. A bold experiment, perhaps, but most castle-builders would not take such a risk.

Guarding the gate

'No fortress is stronger than its weakest part', and the gate, the hole that the builder was forced to leave in the walls, must be that part. This was obvious, and from the earliest castles the builders tried to ensure that it would be as difficult and danger-ous to knock down the gate as to attack any other part of the walls.

The entrance to a keep could be made difficult with stairs and forebuilding (page 11), but the gate in a curtain wall had to be wide, with an approach level enough for horses and carts. How could this be made secure? Some early castles trusted simply in the gate being massive and well barred, but frequently there was a flanking tower close by, preferably to the left (from the defenders' point of view) so that they could shoot at the attackers' right sides, which were not protected by their shields.

An alternative idea was to pass the gate through a tower, so that it became an entrance passage which could be closed at both ends, blocked, and defended from rooms above and at both sides. This seems to be a better arrangement than the gate in the wall, but it did not suit everybody. Bramber in Sussex (diagram, page 8) is an interesting example of what happened with one early castle. About 1100 the owner re-placed the wooden palisade around his bailey with a stone curtain wall. He abandoned the motte, and had only one tower on his curtain wall. This had the gate passage going through it. But it must have proved inconvenient to have the only tower pierced like this, and to be without a keep. A few years later the gate tower was enlarged and turned into a keep, and a new gate was cut through the curtain. Something similar happened at other early castles, such as Richmond in York-shire and Ludlow in Shropshire.

The best solution – if the owner could afford it – was to combine both ideas into a full gatehouse. Here the gate stood

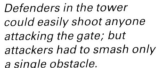

Defenders in the tower could easily shoot anyone attacking the gate; but attackers had to smash only a single obstacle.

Attackers had to force a defended passage with gates at both ends; but defenders had difficulty in covering the ground immediately in front of the gate.

View from side

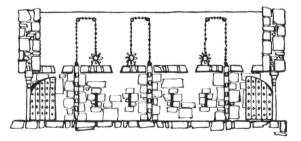

The gatehouse combined the advantages and avoided the disadvantages of the other two arrangements. The longer the passage, the more obstacles could be put in – gates, portcullises, arrow-slits in the walls and 'murder-holes' in the ceiling – besides any drawbridge in front.

23

Types of drawbridge

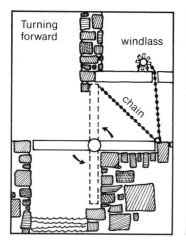

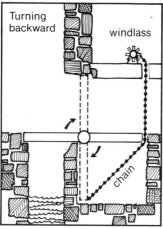

The simplest form of bridge, pivoted at the inner end, is not shown here; we must remember that it was very widely used, especially for small doors and posterns. The balance of these turning bridges could be arranged so that they would naturally rest either in the open or the shut position. In these diagrams, the gates would fall shut if not held open by a strong draw-bar; holes for such bars can still sometimes be seen. The chains to the windlass could be guided by pulleys in whatever direction was most convenient.

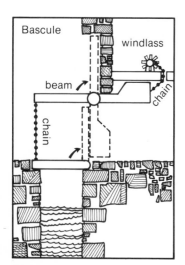

The entrance to the fourteenth-century Breton castle of Montmuran, with its bascule bridges. There are two beams and grooves for the main bridge, one for the footbridge to the right. Because no part of a bascule device lay below road level, it was particularly useful where there was a wet moat rising high. Notice the well-developed machicolations around the top of the gatehouse.

between two towers, and then there was an entrance passage which went through a building that linked the towers. The earliest gatehouses of this sort appeared about the middle of the twelfth century, and henceforward the gatehouse was one of the strongest parts of any large castle.

A gatehouse was not only massively built, it had a whole range of ingenious devices to stop the besiegers from bursting through. Outside the passage there were arrow-slits in the towers to cover the approach, and a machicolation over the entrance – indeed, the earliest machicolations to be found in castles are over the gate. If the attackers got into the passage they would meet a storm of stones, arrows, boiling liquid and spear-thrusts from 'murder-holes' in the roof and arrow-slits in the side walls; and this would be while they were crowded in a helpless tangle, trying to force the next gate or portcullis. Occasionally the passage might have a sharp bend; this would not only tend to confuse the attackers, unable to see clearly in the dim passage, but would allow them no space to heave a battering ram against the final barriers.

The gates themselves were generally thick timber, heavily reinforced with iron, swinging inwards on big iron hinges, held

shut by stout wooden bars drawn across through iron sockets. Sometimes there would be a small door cut into the gate, so that people on foot could get in or out without the great gate having to be opened. Few medieval gates still survive, but a visitor to a castle can often find remains of the hinges, see the deep hole in the stonework at the side of the gate where the draw-bar was pushed when not being used, and identify the stone rim against which the gate would press tightly when shut, so that an attacker could hardly get a lever into the crack. As an extra protection, a heavy iron grille called a *yett* was sometimes fitted in front of the wooden gate, most commonly in Scottish and Irish castles.

In the early twelfth century an additional form of gate came to Britain, the *portcullis*. This was a heavy wooden grille, again bound with iron, that slid up and down instead of swinging on hinges. The garrison could raise and lower it by a windlass in the room above the passage, where the portcullis itself was hoisted when not in use. Very few original portcullises survive, but it is easy to detect where one used to be. Its slot in the roof of the passage may have been blocked up, but the grooves running down the side walls to guide the edges of the portcullis and hold them steady usually remain.

If the castle was surrounded by a moat or a dry ditch there would normally be a drawbridge in front of the gate, and when raised this formed yet another obstacle. As the diagrams show, there were several different ways of working draw-

bridges – or turning bridges, as some types are more accurately termed. Especially effective must have been the sort that had a deep pit behind, into which the inner end of the bridge pivoted. If the moat was very wide there would be a causeway between the castle and the outer bank, and in addition to the drawbridge beside the gate there might be another gap further forward, with another drawbridge.

Formidable as such a gatehouse undoubtedly was, some castle-owners wished to be even more secure, and felt that it was better to prevent an enemy even getting up to the gate. So they built an outwork known as a *barbican*; as early as the reign of William I, one was built in front of the combined keep-gatehouse of Exeter. As the picture of Conisbrough shows (page 26), a barbican is a wall that loops out from the main curtain wall in front of the gatehouse. The gate into the barbican itself had defences, and as time went on these were made more elaborate, with turrets, portcullises and drawbridges, until some barbicans really became outer gatehouses.

As we can see from such examples as Exeter and Bramber, the idea of combining the castle's strongest tower, the keep, with the guarding of the gate occurred to castle-builders quite early. When very powerful gatehouses were developed, the idea of a keep-gatehouse was revived. But this was only part of the great development in castle planning that came during the thirteenth century.

Even where gate and portcullis no longer survive, it is often possible to detect where they once were, inside the gatehouse passage: traces of hinges (H), draw-bar holes (D), portcullis grooves (P). The grooves often stop well above the ground, to catch a shoulder on the side of the portcullis and prevent the spikes crashing into the cobbles. Gates were usually wooden, reinforced with iron, but in Scotland the all-iron yett was fairly common, a lattice gate with bars cleverly interwoven. The yett, only half of which is shown, is at Doune castle (page 30).

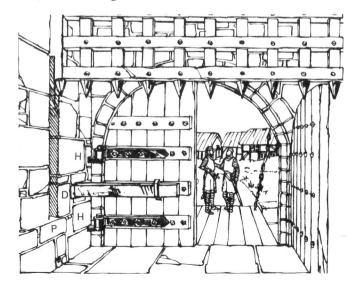 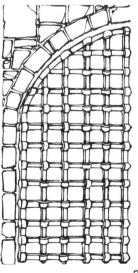

Keep-and-bailey castle development in Britain

Conisbrough, Yorkshire, was entirely rebuilt about 1180–90 by Hamelin Plantagenet, half-brother of Henry II, and this reconstruction gives us a good idea of an up-to-date castle of that time. Note the barbican; the half-round wall-towers carefully sited to give protection where needed; and how the keep is placed on the curtain wall, so as to be in the front line as well as the last stronghold. Compared to Orford (page 18), this keep is completely circular, but with six buttress-turrets.

Pembroke, as it now appears, is probably the work of its most famous owner, William Marshal, soon after 1200. It is larger than Conisbrough and has a more elaborate gatehouse with the adjoining wall doubly thick; the barbican has been largely destroyed. The wall-towers are large and circular. The foundations can be seen of a cross-wall that divided the bailey. The keep, the largest round one in Britain, is placed to support the cross-wall and dominate the bailey, and has a stone dome from which two ranks of archers could shoot simultaneously.

Warkworth, Northumberland, shows many stages of development under different lords. It still has the plan of a motte-and-bailey castle, but the stone walls that replaced the palisade did not include all the original bailey, it seems; a wide 'shelf' can be seen outside the far wall in this air view. The existing walls and towers were built or rebuilt at about the dates marked. The keep is of a highly unusual design, probably unique, and combines strength with luxury and magnificence. About the time it was built the famous Harry Hotspur must often have dwelt in the castle.

Helmsley, Yorkshire, though not associated with great and famous men, has many features to remind us that castle builders were not slavish followers of fashion, but adapted ideas to suit their own circumstances. The earthworks, probably dating from about 1100, do not suggest any sort of motte-and-bailey arrangement. The keep, probably about 1200, is astride the curtain, square on the bailey side but rounded to face an attacker. The great barbican, probably about 1250, shields the whole width of the castle and forms part of the earth rampart, between two ditches, that surrounds the castle, with a smaller barbican at the far end.

Stages in the development of one castle: Brougham, Cumbria

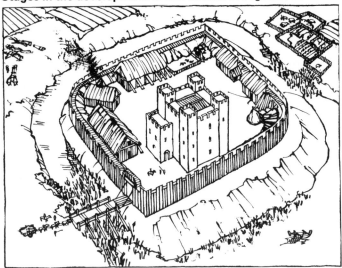

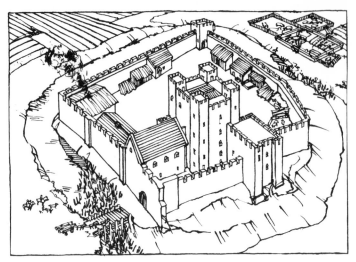

1. About 1170–80, on the site of a Roman fort by the river Eamont, a square stone keep was built within a bailey protected by ditch and palisade. Most of the buildings were wooden.

3. About 1290 a tower was added to the most exposed corner of the curtain wall, the keep was heightened and an inner gatehouse was built between keep and curtain.

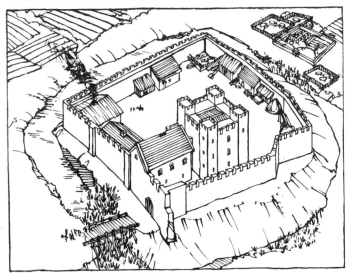

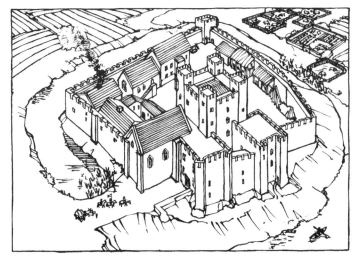

2. During the first half of the thirteenth century a stone residential block was built beside the keep, adjoining the forebuilding. The palisade was replaced by a stone curtain, and within this a stone hall, kitchen, chapel and other buildings were placed.

4. In the early fourteenth century more domestic buildings were added and also an outer gatehouse adjoining the keep. This was heightened a few years later and linked to the inner gatehouse by a passage building.

By about 1330 the castle was in its final form, a compact though rather weak bailey dominated by a powerful keep-and-gatehouse group of buildings.

Frederick, Wonder of the World, and his castles

It is obvious that the problems of designing the best possible castles were occupying some very intelligent people, and the most outstanding of these, probably, was the Holy Roman Emperor Frederick II, nicknamed *Stupor Mundi*, the Wonder of the World, who reigned from 1212 to 1250. He was a man of endless scientific curiosity and experiment, never satisfied with half-explanations or unproven tales, always trying to think out something better. When he applied his mind to designing castles the results were unlike other castles of the time, though he knew about the military architecture of England and France, Germany, Italy and the Holy Land. A German by birth, he lived mostly in Sicily and southern Italy, where he built his famous castles.

It is interesting that at Termoli, for example, he did not choose to build a circular keep. Instead the keep is really a vast plinth, a pyramid with the top cut off flat. From this rises a smaller tower that commands the lower part completely; even if the enemy were to storm the lower part, they could not remain there, without shelter under a hail of missiles from the upper tower.

At another of his castles, Castel del Monte, it is difficult to think in terms of either keep or bailey. The whole structure is a squat, octagonal building with the rooms grouped around a central courtyard, and at each corner an octagonal tower from which archers could cover both the adjoining walls and neighbouring towers.

Castles like these are a warning to us not to try too hard to fit castles into particular types and periods. The classifications we use are only made by historians to help us understand more clearly how various features and designs developed. The builders would doubtless study any new ideas they heard about, but they could not copy from textbooks. They used their common sense and experience, and tried to exploit the advantages and make up for the weaknesses of the ground they had to build on. They bore in mind the main circumstances of this particular castle – was it, for instance, really likely to be heavily attacked? – and how much money was available? Besides, many castles were not created according to a single plan, but altered during several centuries of use. When we look at any castle we have to try to understand what its builder was and was not trying to achieve; most of them were in no position to attempt brilliant experiments like the Emperor Frederick.

The keep at Termoli

Castel del Monte, built about 1240, stands on a crest and its geometrical regularity gives it an appearance of completeness. In fact it was intended to stand within another fortified enclosure, but this was never built. Frederick built equally geometrical rectangular castles.

5 Designing perfect castles

All the improved details described in the last chapter led to an enormous change in the strength and appearance of castles. Even an old keep-and-curtain castle looked quite transformed with its machicolations and wall-towers, its spurs and arrow-slits, and its formidable gatehouse. Such additions were, of course, carefully placed by the castle-owner and his builder. But when it came to building an entirely new castle, a master builder (or architect) now had so many ideas about fortification that he could select and combine different features, giving due weight to different principles of defence, so as to produce a castle that was exactly right for its owner's purposes.

Concentrating the power

In the days when most of the defences of a castle were fairly easy for a determined enemy to penetrate – perhaps only a

Doune, Perthshire, a small castle of the late fourteenth century. The main buildings, blocked together, are the hall (H), lord's private hall and apartments (L), and kitchen (K). The lord's quarters are cut off from the main hall by a strong internal wall, and control the gate passage (G).

palisade, or a simple curtain without towers – it had made excellent sense to have a strong keep. But even then its disadvantages were easy to see. It could not protect most of the people and property in the castle. It could not hold a large garrison, one that would be big enough to threaten the enemy with raids. And if it was true that a handful of men in a Norman keep could hold it against an army, it was equally true that it took only a small force to blockade such a keep. Finally, many keeps were placed in the middle of the bailey. This enabled the people in the keep to dominate all parts of the bailey, but it usually meant that the keep was too far back to help against an enemy attacking the outer walls.

When the curtain wall was made much stronger, was there still any purpose in having a keep? The Framlingham alternative (page 22) proved a failure; the castle put up only a feeble resistance when attacked in 1216, in marked contrast to the doughty resistance of the old keep of Rochester the previous year (page 15) and the triumphant defence of Dover (page 16). But if the curtain walls were to be given a series of really massive towers, would not one of these serve as a keep? There was a great deal to be said for thrusting forward a castle's main strength instead of holding it back. And even if an attacker got over the curtain wall, he would find it far harder to deal with several large towers, all capable of holding out independently, than a single keep.

All the same, many a lord felt happier if he had a special stronghold within his castle, greater than any other tower.

As gatehouses developed it became increasingly obvious that they must be far bigger than the other towers on the curtain wall, and that by enlarging them still further to serve also as keeps, they would be made even more powerful protection for the gate. There was an added advantage, too. The lord and his most reliable people would now be living beside the entrance, next to the mechanism that controlled drawbridge and portcullis. It would thus be harder for traitors to open the gate to the enemy. And it was less expensive to build one specially mighty tower than two.

There could be different opinions about the merits of the keep-gatehouse – perhaps because of the differences between sites. The most famous of all keep-gatehouses, Harlech (page 35), continued virtually unaltered. The keep-gatehouse at Dunstanburgh, which must have been even more impressive than Harlech before it fell into ruin, was soon blocked and

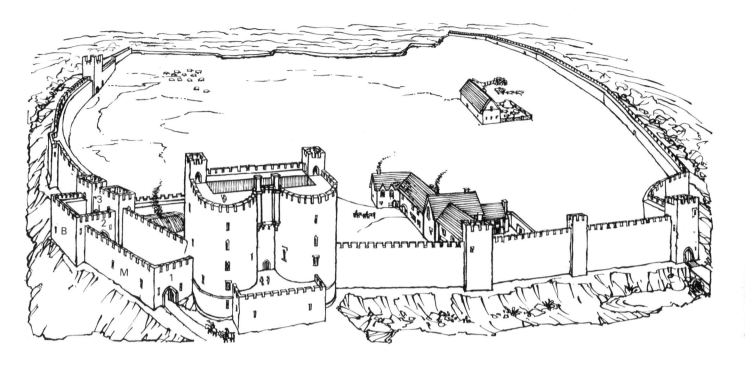

Dunstanburgh castle, Northumberland, was built about 1313–25 on a wide cliff-top site, with a huge keep-gatehouse at the only easy approach. About fifty years later the entrance was altered, as shown in this reconstruction. The barbican was removed and the gate passage blocked by a square forebuilding. Now purely a keep, the great building still

dominated the entrance. A visitor must pass a new outer gate (1); go between the curtain wall and a new mantlet or covering wall (M); pass another gate (2) into the new barbican (B); and turn right through yet another gate (3). Now he was in the vast outer bailey, but still had to enter the small inner bailey before reaching the keep.

became purely a keep, though it still dominated the new entrance to the castle. Even in small castles, lords sometimes thought it wise to concentrate the main strength of the defences over or near the gate, and to live there themselves.

The line of defence

Wherever the lord's special strongpoint might be, the first purpose was to keep an attacker outside the whole castle. As the curtain wall defences improved, it became more likely that a castle-owner could pin his faith on holding a line of defence around his bailey, rather than on having an ultimate refuge. The shorter this line, the easier it would be to defend with a limited garrison, and the closer and stronger the towers that could be afforded with a limited amount of money. But too

short a defence perimeter could mean that there was not enough space within the bailey to shelter the people and animals that were needed.

Sometimes the site itself might be so strong that the enemy could attack from only one direction, and therefore almost all of the builder's efforts could be spent on making an impregnable line of defence here. In their mountain castles the Germans frequently built a *schildmauer* (shieldwall), a huge, wide tower that completely blocked the only path into the castle. In Britain, although many castles were well placed on rocky hills, few stood on sites that could use this device. The exceptions were on headlands where steep cliffs rose from the sea and the only level approach could be blocked by a line of fortified buildings. Such a castle is Tantallon, on a promontory over the Firth of Forth, where not much remains of the weak

defences at the cliff edge, nor of the small walls that crowned the ditches in front, but where the mighty mass of the shieldwall has endured.

No matter how strong the principal line of defences might be, it was better, whenever possible, to try to prevent the enemy from throwing the full force of his attack against it. This could be done by building outer defences. At Chateau Gaillard the site made it possible to compel the enemy to take first an outer bailey, then a second bailey before facing the final, strongest bailey. But often a lord would need to build his castle in a place where the enemy could attack from any direction. Then the defences had to be strong all around. In such a position, the main walls must also be surrounded by a complete ring of outer defences. Such an arrangement is called *concentric*, the geometric name for two circles with the same centre.

Kenilworth is such a castle. Here there are two baileys, the inner one completely inside the outer. Around them both was a wide moat with an artificial lake held in by a fortified dam. In 1266 Kenilworth was the last stronghold where the supporters of the rebel Simon de Montfort still resisted King Henry III. Without hope of relief, it held out for six months against the royal army. The king's engines failed to breach the defences, and when starvation and illness forced the garrison to surrender they were able to get good terms.

Strong as it was, Kenilworth had a great fault. The inner bailey, with its square keep, was so situated within the much larger outer bailey that archers there and on the keep were too far from some of the outer walls to support the men holding them. The Earl of Gloucester fought at the siege of Kenilworth, and shortly afterwards he started to build an equally great castle at Caerphilly, in South Wales. Like Kenilworth, Caerphilly had an artificial lake and two rings of wall. But here the large inner curtain was close to the low—but still very strong—outer one, so that archers on the main wall could shoot down on attackers trying to surmount the first layer of defence. The scheme worked like this: the attacker could not assault the main wall until he had taken the outer one, but he could not take, or at least hold, the outer one while the defenders of the main wall were still active. Logically, therefore, it should be impossible to take a properly planned concentric castle.

Not only were the distance between the two lines of defence and their relative height kept carefully balanced, but there was

Two methods of blocking the enemy's advance. Tantallon, built in the late fourteenth century on a headland jutting into the Firth of Forth, has a sort of schildmauer, *with a tower at each end and a gatehouse in the centre. Château Gaillard, built 1195–8 on a cliff by the river Seine, has a keep (K), inside an inner bailey (IB) and middle bailey (MB). The only practicable approach is blocked by the formidable outer bailey (OB) and its deep ditches.*

Concentric defences using water

At Kenilworth, Warwickshire, the plan of the castle that held out so well in 1266 can still be seen clearly, despite considerable later rebuilding. The keep is at one corner of a rough square of buildings that mark the position of the inner bailey, standing in the middle of a large outer bailey. These concentric lines of defence were themselves protected by a large lake that prevented mining; this is now drained, but its position has been marked on the photograph.

At Caerphilly, South Wales, the castle did not develop gradually like Kenilworth, but was built within four years, 1268–71, by a baron who had been at the siege of Kenilworth. It has the same strengths, but is improved, up-to-date. The compact, symmetrical inner bailey has lofty walls, big towers, no keep but two large gatehouses. It stands inside an outer bailey with walls so low and so close to the inner curtain that an attacker might perhaps mount them but could never survive there. All around lay the elaborate water defences of the great lake, partly dammed and regulated by an enormous barbican stretching across one end.

also a regularity and evenness about the design of the castle as a whole. Cut down the middle, the two halves would have been practically identical. In other words, the castles had been designed to be *symmetrical*.

This was not just to look neat. Architects understood that if a castle presented the same arrangement of defences all the way around, it would be difficult for an attacker to select any point that seemed to have some special feature which might be turned into a weakness. The Emperor Frederick had followed the idea about as far as it could be taken at Castel del Monte (page 29), but the symmetrical castles of the late thirteenth century were probably not copied from this. Rather they were the final development of increasingly skillful castle planning over many years.

The North Wales castles of Edward I

The most perfectly designed castles ever built in Britain—and, some would claim, in Europe too—were those that Edward I built to keep a tight grip on North Wales after he had conquered that land of mountains and fiery warriors. They showed all the most advanced principles: great gatehouses and wall-towers, concentric and symmetrical plans, expertly situated arrow-slits and never a right angle to be battered or mined. Yet all are different, to suit the sites chosen. The master builder might decide to dispense with an outer wall, or even a gatehouse, if he thought that it would not be helpful. Most of these castles were designed to protect new walled towns with inhabitants loyal to Edward, and all could be supplied by sea, for the English king could always get ships and Welsh rebels could not.

Were such magnificent castles really necessary, though? The Welsh were famed for their sudden and furious attacks, but they had no skill in sieges. Perhaps these mighty buildings were intended to impress the Welsh with a sense of Edward's power, and make them feel that rebellion was hopeless. Therefore the castles were made far grander than the little keeps which had contented the Welsh princes. We cannot be certain. Edward's builder was a man from Savoy, Master James of St. George. When we look at these superb works, we may even suspect that both king and architect loved castles, and used the conquest of North Wales as an opportunity to build the most magnificent they could conceive.

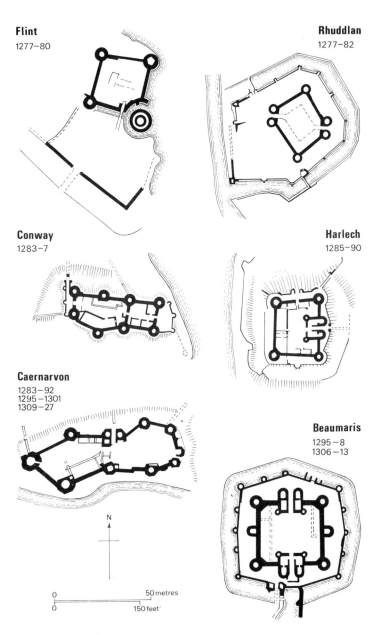

The six main Edwardian castles of North Wales. The plans are to the same scale, to make comparison easier. Pictures of the earliest two are on page 22 and the front cover, the 'big four' opposite. Each was designed to fit its own particular site, yet all show similar understanding and skill.

The great Edwardian castles

Both Conway (left) and Caernarvon (right) are high-walled, multi-towered castles, with a division across the single bailey. Both are palaces as well as fortresses, and both dominate the walled ports in which they stand. But Conway stands high on a rock, has two barbicans but no gatehouses. Caernarvon occupies a lower site, had a wet moat and two very strong gatehouses without barbicans. From the outside, Caernarvon looks almost new, with its striped walls intended to impress. Conway has lost the roofs shown in the reconstruction drawing of the castle when new, but otherwise looks just as mighty.

Harlech (left) and Beaumaris (right), from their plans, also seem to be very similar. Yet one of the pair stands on a rocky hill high above the sea, the other on flat ground beside a low shore. The sea has receded from beneath Harlech's rock, but otherwise the castle has changed little from the way it looked in the Middle Ages, as shown in the reconstruction drawing. It proved its strength in some famous sieges. Beaumaris, in a weaker position, had an even stronger design, but it was never really tested, nor even finished.

6 The castle as a house to live in

So far we have mainly looked at castles as fortresses, as if the builders' only concern was to make them safe against attack. Thus we were able to explain the changing designs of castles in terms of military developments. But if security was the first concern, there was also the problem of fitting inside the defences all the buildings needed for the daily life of the lord, his family and its servants. The greater the lord, the more people he would have in his household. Besides being a home where he could live in comfort and maintain the dignity necessary to impress other people with his importance and power, the castle had to be the headquarters of an extensive estate. From here the lord's officials supervised many villages, and even towns, ensuring that they paid rents and fees fully and punctually. There had to be room for these officials to work and keep their accounts; also, since many of the rents were paid in goods rather than in money, there had to be plenty of storage space – though barns and cellars for food and drink would have been needed anyway to supply a large household, especially if there were any danger of being besieged. In addition, the lord would usually be responsible for keeping order and enforcing justice in his lands; the king would probably reserve major crimes, where a convicted criminal could lose life or limb, for his own courts, but the lord's courts would deal with lesser crimes and settle disputes between his tenants. So the castle must have a room impressive enough for trials, and a place to keep court records. This was all normal routine. Sometimes, though, important guests – perhaps even the king himself – would arrive with their followers, and there must be arrangements to entertain them in noble fashion. An architect had to bear all this in mind while planning what buildings should be included inside the defences and how far, for instance, a tower could be used for storage as well as kept ready for fighting.

Conditions would vary enormously. Castles on the Welsh Marches or the Anglo-Scottish Border would have to be ready for battle at short notice, while castles in the centre of a well-governed kingdom might never have to withstand an attack. Some castles were the permanent homes of their lords, but others belonged to great men who held many castles, and travelled often from one to another. In these castles there would be separate lodgings for the constable who governed for most of the time, as well as for the lord who arrived from time to time with his train of servants and men-at-arms to see how well his estates were prospering, decide any questions that were too important to be settled by his local officials, and eat up the food that had been collected as rent. At such times even the most peaceful castle must have been crowded and bustling.

The great hall was still the central room, as it had been from the earliest times. Even if, in the later Middle Ages especially,

The hall of Penshurst Place, Kent, built in the 1340s, still keeps many medieval features. This view is from the lord's end of the hall opposite the screens. From the central hearth warmth and light could spread all around, while the smoke from the blazing logs rose and left through a louvre in the high roof.

the lord often found it too much trouble to eat in the hall regularly with all his people, there were many occasions—the great holidays of Christmas, Easter and Pentecost, for instance, or when important guests were staying at the castle—when the lord would dine in state. The hall would be full of his retainers with himself very obviously at their head, and the meal might have a dozen or more courses, served with much ceremony. The more distinguished the guests, the more varied and elaborate would be the dishes set before them.

The kitchens capable of providing such feasts had to be large and fairly near the hall. Because of the fire risk, builders had to try to make them both safe and convenient for serving; at Caerphilly they placed the main kitchen outside the wall of the inner bailey, and made a door in the curtain wall for the servants carrying food to the hall. Some kitchens had high, pointed roofs which allowed more draft for the fires and air for the people working there—hot, smelly work as the food was cooked over large open fires in the middle of the kitchen or, later, at equally large fireplaces with chimneys against the walls. Sometimes there would be an oven at the side of a fireplace, but often the bakehouse and brewhouse were separate buildings—bread and ale were the usual food and drink of ordinary people, and the castle would need a good, steady supply of both. Near the kitchen there would be a store for ale and wine, the *buttery*. There would be separate passages from the kitchen and buttery to one end of the great hall, cut off from the rest by screens, where the food and drink were brought to those who had to carry them to the tables.

The lord's dais (page 7) would normally be at the far end of the hall from the screens, and here he would have a door leading to his private rooms. His main sitting-room was called the *solar*, because it would whenever possible have south-facing windows to catch the sunlight. There were also bed-chambers for the lord and his family and some personal servants. In the later Middle Ages the lord would take most of his meals in his private apartments, with only a few people, and the food would usually be prepared in a fairly small kitchen nearby. A really great lord, however, could not avoid a good deal of ceremony even here, as we can see from the way the artists of the fifteenth century depicted scenes in the households of the high nobility; nothing less would have been thought suitable for a man of such rank.

By present-day standards most rooms, even in the lord's

Cooks chopping, mixing and boiling food; early 14th century.

apartments, would seem very sparsely furnished. In the later Middle Ages, most people would have a bed, but only the rich a chair; most sat on stools, benches or seats carved in walls, usually beside windows. Tables were still mainly of the trestle type. One reason why there were so few large permanent pieces of furniture may have been the difficulty of carrying them up spiral staircases and through narrow doorways. Many things besides tables were designed to be dismantled and reassembled as required. This made good sense especially for a lord who travelled a great deal; for instance, it was better to keep clothes in a chest that could be transported than in a clumsy cupboard. Any large permanent furnishings that were thought necessary might have to be built where they were to stay. There was no such problem about floor coverings, but because they would soon become very dirty it was better to use mats of braided rushes or straw which could be replaced easily

Armourers at work on helmets, horse mail and a sword.

An everyday scene in a castle bailey; artist's reconstruction of Framlingham (page 22) in the thirteenth century.

common to cover the walls with plaster and paint on it; sometimes there would be religious themes, sometimes stories from Greek and Roman mythology (with the characters dressed as medieval knights and ladies, for medieval artists showed no concern about historical accuracy), sometimes patterns of animals and flowers, or mythical beasts, or abstract designs. When you stand in the bare stone rooms of an uninhabited castle, you have to make a real effort to imagine them as they really were, ablaze with colour all over the walls and ceilings. Remember, too, that the nobles would be dressed in rich robes, often with furs and jewels; their servants would wear colourful clothes, often in their lord's livery; the men-at-arms would glitter with burnished steel. That was how a great castle looked when its lord was in residence. Many castles also had their outer walls whitewashed, so that from a distance they shone bright and clean.

To maintain all this there had to be hard work, efficient organisation and plentiful supplies. The stores in the cellars must be used while they were still good, and constantly replenished. Fresh food could be brought straight from gardens and orchards, fishponds and rabbit warrens that lay within the castle's defences or just outside. Many castles had dovecotes, sometimes looking like towers but with the inner walls full of recesses where the birds nested; they provided pigeon pie even in midwinter, when other fresh meat was difficult to find. To grind grain there would perhaps be a windmill on a high place; at the Tower of London there was a water mill powered by the rise and fall of the tide in the moat.

Cleanliness was very important in a place where so many people might be living close together. Water could sometimes be brought from a nearby stream, but wells within the castle itself were essential. Wherever possible, there would be a well inside the keep, but there was also a need for a well in the bailey where it would be more convenient for people working in the stables, the smithy, the laundry and all the other workshops. Probably most ordinary people got a complete bath only if they plunged into the stream on hot summer days, but for the upper classes there were tubs which their servants filled with hot water; at meal times the servants brought round ewers for the ladies and gentlemen to rinse their fingers after picking up food—there were no forks.

As to sanitation, the builders might arrange for garderobes (page 10) to empty into the moat, but more usually they dis-

and cheaply—and which could also be very good-looking and hard-wearing. Sometimes people simply strewed on their floor loose rushes—easier still to replace. Only a few rich men at the end of the Middle Ages boasted cloth carpets, and these were more often spread on tables and walls than on floors.

If the owners of the castles did not care greatly for furniture, they often made up for it by decorating their walls. Coloured hangings, sometimes embroideries or tapestries, were draped all around some rooms; not only did they look pleasant, but they reduced drafts and softened noise—both serious problems in large stone buildings. As an alternative, it was

Musicians playing the harp, the psaltery (a kind of zither where the strings were plucked with a goose quill), the oliphaunt (a trumpet made of a hollowed tusk) and two types of vielle (the ancestor of the modern violin and 'cello); 13th century.

The chapel in Dover keep, so elaborately carved and small that it may have been used by only a few important people.

charged into a cess-pit which somebody would have to clean out from time to time, possibly carting away the contents to fertilise fields.

Amidst all their day-to-day tasks, medieval people were not allowed to forget their religious duties. No major castle was complete without at least one chapel, in the keep, or in a wall-tower, or standing by itself in the bailey. There would be priests to serve here, often with their living-rooms near the chapel. The lord would worship with his people, much as he dined in the hall; and here too he sometimes preferred to be private, so that we see in some castles, such as Beaumaris, small rooms by the chapel from which it was possible to see mass being celebrated without being seen by the rest of the congregation. It was also quite common for the lord or his lady to have a tiny room for praying, or oratory, next to their bedrooms.

In essentials, castle life would have been much the same all through the Middle Ages. But, just as ideas on warfare and defence developed and affected the design of castles, so did trade and wealth and people's ideas about comfort and luxury, not to mention fashion and ceremonial. The demand for more and finer suites of rooms for the lord and lady and their rela-

tives and honoured guests, and better service for them, gave the master builder extra problems. It all took space, which is one reason why some of the later castles are so large, and a sprawling castle is not usually as strong as a compact one. Lords and ladies naturally preferred to be able to move about easily; but a castle designed to allow this also allowed an attacker to move easily once he had burst in. Large windows, perhaps beautifully carved, were delightful in peace; but, even with wooden shutters and iron bars, they were a weakness in war. So, in the later Middle Ages especially, the castle-builder might have to struggle to reconcile the conflicting demands of comfort and safety.

Royal castles were particularly likely to need stately accommodation. Edward I's castles in North Wales were mostly planned with space for a royal household. Caernarvon particularly seems to have been designed as a palace-castle (pages 34–5), yet there were no windows in the more exposed walls, not even for a royal suite. Until the end of the Middle Ages, when castles lost their military value, even the most palatial remained formidable.

Finally, what of the castle as a prison? Some people cherish a grisly vision of every castle basement as a place of skeletons and rats, chains and instruments of torture; the word *donjon* has become *dungeon*. The truth behind this lurid notion is that a castle sometimes was used as the local jail; this often happened after the end of its military usefulness, and the same fate befell town fortifications such as London's Newgate. During the Middle Ages it is probable that the lord, like anybody enforcing law and order, sometimes had to lock people up, and a tower or cellar in his castle might well be the most secure place. Some castles have small 'pits' or 'bottle dungeons' where the only entrance was in the roof; this seems to be more common in areas of lawlessness, such as the Anglo-Scottish Border. Such prisons are often beside a guard-room or porter's lodge, and would be convenient, secure lock-ups for dangerous outlaws that had just been caught. In the Middle Ages, ordinary people were not usually imprisoned for long; offenders would be fined or punished physically. Important people were sometimes held captive for long periods, but usually in comfort, often more like guests than prisoners. Admittedly, people in positions of power sometimes turned out to be corrupt and cruel, and horrifying deeds were commonplace in war; but there is nothing specially medieval about that.

7 The smaller castles

In the last few chapters we have been looking mainly at powerful castles belonging to kings or great lords. The reason is that these set the standards for others to follow. Also, the big castles have often lasted better than the small and are better known—indeed, they often attract crowds of visitors. But most castles belonged to people who could not afford anything so grand, though they wanted something that would be reasonably secure and imposing. Most landowners in most European countries built whatever they judged best for their own circumstances, and the result was a multitude of castles of all shapes and sizes. They are so varied that it would scarcely be possible to classify them completely; nevertheless, it is useful to recognise some of the most popular types.

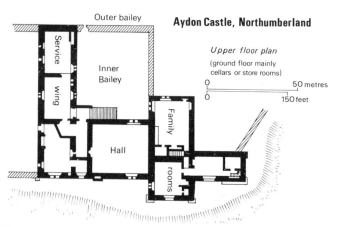

Aydon Castle, Northumberland

Outer bailey

Inner Bailey

Service wing

Hall

Family rooms

Upper floor plan
(ground floor mainly cellars or store rooms)

0   50 metres
0   150 feet

The fortified manor house

An ordinary knight or squire, lord of one village or perhaps two, could not aspire to a big castle. Yet he needed a house where he could keep up some dignity as lord of the manor, hold his manor court, store his records, and protect himself and his family from robbery and riot. The danger of attacks would be greater in some areas, borderlands for example, but might arise anywhere at times of disturbance and distress—such as famines—or when the king was too weak to prevent feuds and revolts.

What was the least that a small lord could manage with? The minimum was a hall, kitchen, private rooms, stable and a few store-sheds; in other words, the basic accommodation of a castle, but on a small scale. If these were arranged around a yard and a battlement wall built around them, that might be enough especially since a ditch or moat could add a little extra protection. It might be as much as the owner could afford, but his son or grandson might be able to strengthen the place with a gatehouse and a tower or two. Many a small castle consists of such parts, erected how and when the lord saw fit.

A contrast in manor houses. Aydon, Northumberland, built around 1300, began as a hall on the edge of a cliff, to which a service wing and battlemented inner bailey were soon added; the outer bailey was a farmyard. Maxstoke, Warwickshire (above) was built about 1350 in flat, rich, peaceful country; note the symmetrical design, the dignity.

The 'four-square' castle

By the fourteenth and fifteenth centuries most countries of western Europe were well supplied with castles, and for most lords there was no need to do more than repair and improve the castles they had inherited. Some, though, still wanted new ones. Perhaps they had recently become rich, and wished to show the world that they were men of importance, or perhaps they had reason to think there was special danger of raids. A good number of those who, in several countries, built medium-sized castles at this time followed a plan that was compact, symmetrical, convenient for living in and at the same time easy to defend.

Such a castle would consist of strong curtain walls forming a square or rectangle, with a tower at each corner. These cur-tains were also the back walls of the residential buildings, so that the inside of the castle was not a bailey containing many separate structures, but a courtyard completely enclosed by continuous ranges that rose as high as the rampart walk. By good planning the builder could bring everything close together, without cramping but without wasting space, and so provide a pleasant residence; while the outside gave very reassuring protection.

Castles of this sort were popular in Spain, the Netherlands and Britain. In Spain some of them had outer defences that turned them into concentric castles. In the Netherlands it was often easy to surround the castle with a wide wet moat or even a lake, crossed only by a causeway. Even without such extra precautions, these neat castles would prove tough nuts for anything less than a big, fully equipped army to crack.

A contrast in 'four-square' castles. Bolton castle, Yorkshire, represents a plain, strong style that was popular in northern England. Four compact ranges of living and working rooms, three storeys high, fortified on the outer face and reasonably defensible on the courtyard side, have four large, business-like towers projecting from the corners. Such castles usually had no outer defences but were well sited on clear ground that gave no cover to an attacker. The gate at Bolton can be seen tucked in the angle covered by the front left tower. Maxstoke (opposite) shares the square plan but lacks the uninterrupted ranges of buildings and warlike appearance.

Muiden, Holland, lies in flat, waterlogged country, and adapts the square plan to fit the conditions. Within a wide moat, it has a high, dominant gatehouse and corner towers, these being round. The curtain walls are relatively low, though well crenellated; there are no ranges of buildings in the Bolton style, but a high-roofed hall can be seen at the far side. In some respects this plan is more similar to Maxstoke, but stronger. Both Bolton and the present structure at Muiden were built about 1380, but the Dutch castle is of brick. By this time the Netherlands people, short of good stone, had become expert brickmakers, and many of their castles were brick-built.

The tower-house

Several of the 'four-square' castles are to be seen in northern England, where there was always the danger of attacks from Scotland. This was especially so after the attempt to conquer Scotland begun by Edward I of England, which left a legacy of bitter hostility on both sides of the Border. Even when the two kingdoms were at peace, noblemen on both sides might raid. And even when the nobles were quiet, lawless Borderers were always ready to seek plunder – from unprotected people of their own nation as well as the other. So everyone who could lived in a tower, and if they could not afford this they tried to build their houses strongly of stone, with small windows. What the raiders wanted was the cattle, and it was essential to find some means of keeping them safe. A few valuable animals, probably horses, might be sheltered in the bottom storey of the tower, but for the herd generally there would be a yard next to the tower, sometimes with a protected gate. Such an enclosure was called a *barmkin* or *pele*, sometimes spelt *peel*; the latter word means a palisaded enclosure, and on the Border the towers were called pele towers.

These tower-houses were often small, but they included many of the features of larger castles. In the tower there would often be a hall on the middle floor, with rooms for the lord and his family above and storage below. Like a small bailey, the barmkin would often contain barn, stable, workshop and perhaps cottages for servants. Some barmkins had small corner-towers or turrets.

Most medieval tower-houses were plain rectangles in shape, but in Scotland during the sixteenth and seventeenth centuries a number of more complex plans were developed. One reason was that by this time the owners wanted to make full use of hand firearms, and of the small pieces of artillery that even minor lords seem to have owned; so towers were built with projections that allowed gunners to fire along the sides of the main building. A second reason was simply to have more space to live in; this need led to extra turrets, and sometimes the growth of extra rooms at the top which overhung and gave the tower a top-heavy appearance. Indeed, the tops of tower-houses were now commonly roofed over and used as bedrooms, because people who relied on using firearms from gunports, loopholes and windows did not find battlements very useful.

Scotland and northern England were not by any means the

Elphinstone

Scottish tower-houses remained simple stone rectangles throughout the Middle Ages. Elphinstone, East Lothian, built about 1440 and recently demolished, was a good example of the larger sort; it had only one unusual feature, a large number of small rooms in the thickness of the wall. At that period some towers had projecting turrets or wings added, but this seems to have been to provide extra living space, not to improve the defensive plan.

It was when hand-guns became efficient, in the sixteenth century, that tower-builders saw the value of such projections as positions from which loopholes could cover the main walls and door. Claypotts, near Dundee, has a Z plan, with its two rounded turrets projecting from diagonally opposite corners of the square main building. It was built 1569–88.

Claypotts

Craigievar

The palatial tower of Craigievar, Aberdeenshire, was built in the 1620s, and its Renaissance balustrade fits oddly among the pointed Gothic bartizans, those small round roof turrets which Scottish builders loved. Craigievar follows what is called the stepped L plan; the door is in a narrow turret that fits within the angle of the L so as to be protected by both wings.

only places where tower-houses were common. The idea of a small tower is a fairly obvious one for somebody who wants security without great expense. There were tower-houses in many parts of medieval Europe and far beyond. In some areas of West Africa and southern Arabia, for example, people still prefer houses of this type. However, few new tower-houses were being built in Europe during the sixteenth century; they were not needed where people felt that the government was now able to protect them and their property against serious disorder. Scots went on building tower-houses because their government was often too weak to provide such a guarantee.

Tower-houses were commonest of all in Ireland. The reasons for this are not entirely clear, but probably the main one was that government was even less reliable here than in Scotland, and minor lords had even more need to look after themselves. Cattle-stealing was an ancient and almost respectable habit in Ireland, and a lord needed a tower with a yard—*bawn* was the name for it in Ireland—to keep both his own cows and those he might have collected from someone else. For more than a thousand years previously, Irish farmers had lived in *raths*, circular enclosures of earth and wood. It is likely that in the fourteenth and fifteenth centuries those who were rich enough took the idea of a stone tower from the castles of their Anglo-Norman invaders and adapted it to their own requirements.

As they had to do the same job, it is not surprising that, on the whole, Irish tower-houses look rather like Scottish ones. There are some differences. The Irish favoured a 'stepped' pattern of merlon, no more efficient than the plain type but intended to make the tower more handsome. Towers usually have simple rectangular plans—or sometimes circular—but a few late examples, more house than tower, have square or round turrets at each corner, making them look rather like small 'four-square' castles. When owners wanted more accommodation they usually did not build bigger towers, but preferred to add a mansion to the existing tower or build one inside the bawn.

A few Irish were still building fortified houses after the middle of the seventeenth centuries, and they were probably the last genuine castle-builders in Europe. For Ireland was exceptional. In richer and less troubled countries changes had taken place, many years before, that had meant the end of real castles.

Behamore

In Ireland over three thousand tower-houses were built between the beginning of the fourteenth century and the middle of the seventeenth. Most were simple rectangular towers with bawns around or beside them, and they are usually difficult to date. Behamore, County Tipperary, is one of this sort. The drawing is based on a reconstruction model, and shows it with white-washed walls and thatched roof, common features in Irish castles. Its bawn is an old rath re-used, topped by a wattle palisade.

Dunsoghly, near Dublin, built in the middle of the fifteenth century, is one of Ireland's few really large tower-houses. It has almost the look of an earlier keep-and-bailey castle, with its corner turrets and a stonewalled bawn where a chapel stands.

Dunsoghly

Synone

Some towers were round. Synone, in Tipperary, is a sixteenth-century example with four small machicolations sticking out from the parapet. The windows would have been protected by iron bars.

8 The decline of the castle

Hurstmonceux in Sussex is a 'four-square' castle built in the middle of the fifteenth century. At first sight it is very impressive. But is it really the castle's strength, or perhaps an illusion of strength, or simply the beauty of its appearance that impresses? It was a sign of the changing times. In many parts of Europe, lords who were building new castles or, more often, altering old ones were much more interested in comfort and show than in defence. Why were they ceasing to value what they had considered so important for hundreds of years?

Gunpowder

The most obvious answer is guns. Nobody knows who invented gunpowder, but it seems to have reached Europe from the East. The first guns were made in the early fourteenth century, and they were little more than noisy novelties to startle the enemy and frighten their horses. But they soon improved. By the middle of the fifteenth century guns had largely replaced the older forms of artillery in attacking castles. Large guns, called *bombards*, could hammer holes in walls while smaller pieces cleared the battlements.

There was no doubt that guns could be very effective. In 1405 the Scots in Berwick surrendered after the first shot from Henry IV's monster gun had shaken their wall, and in 1449 the French king's train of artillery forced the English out of their castles in Normandy in a much shorter time than it had taken Henry V to capture them, thirty years before. Yet cannon were far from infallible. Few English castles had to face them until the Civil War in the middle of the seventeenth century, and even against the improved guns of that time some castles – Bolton was one – resisted well. Perhaps those Civil War guns were not of the heaviest type, since big guns like bombards were expensive, and very difficult to transport. The kings of Scotland in the later fifteenth century had a very fine train of guns, but sometimes could not manage to bring the heavy pieces into action despite hiring workmen specially to smooth the roads.

Hurstmonceux castle, Sussex, was built of brick, not for lack of stone, as in the Netherlands, but because by the mid-fifteenth century brick was becoming a fashionable material. It has towers and battlements, arrow-slits and some carefully-designed gunports, but the graceful proportions and the many windows and chimneys (though some were added later) reveal its main purpose.

Guns, then, did not suddenly make castles obsolete. At first it seemed that castles could be equipped with guns themselves, and from the late fourteenth century gunports were cut in the walls of some castles. A gunport was normally a round hole, often with a long upright slit or a cross-slit above it; the slit may have been partly for aiming, but was probably more useful for shooting with bows, which were still much better than guns for hitting men. These ports could take only small guns, but in the last stages of the Hundred Years' War (1337–1453) the owners of some French castles built low earthen platforms, or *boulevards*, in front of their walls to protect them from enemy shot and to mount heavy guns of their own.

It was not until later in the fifteenth century that people thought it necessary to build new castles specially designed to resist heavy guns. One of the first such castles is Ravenscraig, Fife, built by James II of Scotland, whose great hobby was guns. Builders had always tried to make castle walls and towers high to give them advantages over attackers, but James saw that this made them a more vulnerable target for guns. To resist cannon, walls must be thicker, not taller. Ravenscraig is similar in its general plan to Tantallon (page 32) but the great wall that cuts off the headland is massive rather than lofty. The upper floors are particularly strong, to mount a large number of guns, and some of these were aimed through square gun-

This illustration from a German book on explosives, dated about 1450, is clumsy but clear. The siege cannon is firing from a four-wheeled carriage which has a chest for ammunition or tools, and is fitted with a shaft for two horses. (In fact, many more horses, hitched in front of the pair at the shaft, would have been needed.) The crossbows and handguns of the other attackers and defenders seem puny in comparison, though the care with which the artist has shown a bulge in the crossbow bolts may mean that they are carrying incendiary material.

ports that gave a much wider field of fire than the old sort. In front was a deep ditch so cut that the enemy could neither see nor shoot at the lower part of the wall until they came to the lip of the ditch.

Ravenscraig was still a true castle, meant to be lived in – it has rooms for the Queen of Scotland. But once the idea was accepted that an up-to-date fortification had to be designed firstly to stand up to heavy gunfire and also to fire back with batteries of equally heavy guns, the buildings that resulted could make little provision for comfortable living. In Renaissance Italy engineers experimented with new styles of 'castle' that had tremendously solid walls, sloping, angled or curved to resist and deflect shot. When Henry VIII of England – guns were among his hobbies, too – decided to build a chain of 'castles' on the south coast to guard against French attacks, he followed such ideas and made them low and rounded. Though what remain of these fortifications are named 'castles', and though Walmer is now an official residence, these were not truly castles. They were purely artillery forts, and nobody could call such a place his home.

Ravenscraig castle, Fife, was built at about the same time as Hurstmonceux, but for very different purposes. This view is from one end of the bottom of the rock-cut ditch. The dotted line shows where the bridge would have been, at ground level.

Deal castle, Kent, one of Henry VIII's string of defences against French attacks on the south coast of England, was built in 1539–40. This print, dating from the middle of the seventeenth century, shows it still in its original state. The stumpy 'keep' is girdled by two tiers of semi-circular bastions, and instead of battlements they are all topped by thick, rounded parapets with embrasures for the batteries of guns.

The king's peace

It is no accident that our examples of castles becoming artillery forts were the property of kings. Only kings could afford such works, and only kings could afford complete trains of artillery with guns of the latest design and largest size. In many European countries the power and wealth of the king was becoming supreme as the Middle Ages ended. Recalcitrant nobles would normally stand no chance against the royal army, and their castles could no longer afford them a secure retreat.

In the past, kings had often permitted lords to build castles to keep order in the land or to protect it against invasion. Now this was not necessary. The king was strong enough to do both jobs with his own men, and anyway castles were losing their value in war – though they might still have a use against peasant revolts. Sometimes a castle might be in such a position that it was worth erecting new artillery defences around it. But as methods of warfare developed in the sixteenth and seventeenth centuries, and the kings of Europe's leading nation-states found it necessary to keep standing armies of professional soldiers, castles proved too small to play much part in the defence of a country; only a well-fortified town would be big enough to hold the garrison and guns needed to resist a modern regular army.

In every way the castle was losing its military value; it was no longer even useful in protecting its lord against other lords. The 'new monarchs' were well able to prevent the armed quarrels between barons that had often broken out in earlier centuries. As royal government extended its grasp the chances of serious revolts among the peasants also seemed less and less. Conditions might vary from country to country, or between different areas in the same kingdom, but generally noblemen came to the conclusion that it was better not to live in strongholds any longer.

Wide windows, broad sweeping staircases, terraces and gardens were far more pleasant than the old walls and towers, picturesque though they had been. Besides, fashions were changing, and no nobleman who wanted to remain respected would risk being thought old-fashioned, poor or miserly; he was expected to keep up his position in society by living in suitable state. The king and the king's ministers expected it, too. No monarch would wish to lower his own dignity by favouring

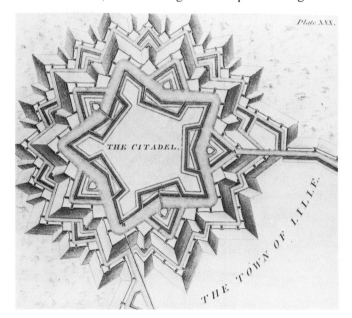

Military engineers developed complex patterns of angular earthworks, sometimes faced with stone, as being best for both using and resisting gunfire. This is an eighteenth-century plan of the citadel of Lille, designed by the greatest French engineer, Vauban (1633–1707).

Attempts were sometimes made to turn old castles into new forts. Twelfth-century Carisbrooke, Isle of Wight, with its shell keep and curtain wall, was given earth ramparts and bastions (at the corners) between 1587 and 1600, when Queen Elizabeth I feared Spanish invasion attempts.

Longford, Wiltshire. The original part is also late Elizabethan. It is triangular with corner towers; the buildings to the right are later additions. But a comparison with Caerlaverock (title page) reveals it to be in fact no more than a splendid country house, virtually defenceless behind its garden and unprotected door.

Where Border raids were a recent memory, landowners often kept their tower houses while adding more comfortable and fashionable wings. This eighteenth-century print of Belsay castle, Northumberland, shows the fourteenth-century tower, a Jacobean manor house added in 1614, and an early Georgian wing built on to that about a century later. (Later still, between 1810 and 1817, an entirely new house was built nearby; following the Greek classical style in fashion then, it was made to look rather like an ancient temple.)

anyone who did not have the right style. Sometimes there was another reason too. Keeping up with fashion, in building as in clothes and furnishings, cost a great deal of money and occupied a lot of time; these nobles were less likely to cause trouble for the king.

Stately homes and ancient monuments

The castle lost its value because of changes in the weapons and methods of war, in political power and in the attitudes and fashions of society. Great changes like these did not happen all together and suddenly. The decline of the castle, therefore, was slow and uneven.

Some castles hardly declined at all, though their importance may have been different. Windsor remained a principal royal residence; it was still very much a castle, with its shell keep between a pair of long baileys, while inside it became more and more a palace. The Tower of London continued as an arsenal, a state prison and a landmark that nobody would have dreamed of destroying. Many other royal castles continued as stores or prisons or, more rarely, garrisons. Some still are;

Edinburgh castle held out for King George while the Jacobite rebels controlled the city in 1745, and remains a military headquarters to the present day.

Sometimes castles were adapted to more comfortable styles of living. There might be new windows, doors and floors in old towers, and new wings adjoining old strongholds. Sometimes a new house would be built within the bailey of an old castle, and sometimes the castle was abandoned and used as a quarry for building stones or roof lead. The Dukes of Northumberland, for example, converted Alnwick castle into a splendid country residence, allowed nearby Warkworth castle to decay and kept a stately mansion, Sion House, near London.

Great houses were still built for great men—some of them new nobles who had risen to wealth and power and title by serving the king, and who did not possess ancestral lands and castles. At first there was a strong tradition that any great house ought to have something of the appearance of a castle. We can see that in Hampton Court at the beginning of the Tudor period. By the time of the Stuarts, however, fashions had changed so that battlements and towers had gone, even as ornaments.

In 1819 Scott's Ivanhoe *set the 'Norman' fashion. In 1820 the owner of Penrhyn, North Wales, having made a fortune from slate quarries, decided to transform his old house into a castle. The architect must have admired Rochester (page 15).*

Still the idea that a castle was somehow a finer thing than a house lingered. Even in the eighteenth century, the great age of classical ideals in art and architecture, when the Middle Ages were disdained as ignorant and uncouth, some of the most outstanding works of the leading architects could still be called castles. It was incongruous, but the French and Germans were doing just the same, calling anything from a modest country mansion to a palace like Versailles a *château* or *schloss*.

Meanwhile there were people, even in the enlightened eighteenth century, who found 'Gothick' ruins 'romantic'. In the early nineteenth century this attitude spread, became fashionable and eventually dominated the art, literature and music of western Europe. The Romantic Revival, as it has been named, brought the Middle Ages into favour. Their imaginations enriched with the tales of Sir Walter Scott, people saw castles as full of bold, bad barons, knights in shining armour, fair ladies and damsels in distress. It became fashionable to adorn houses once more with battlements and even towers or turrets; you can find this sort of thing on large Victorian country houses, suburban villas and middle-class terraces. A few very wealthy people went much further. Some

rebuilt ruined castles and furnished them in what they thought was medieval style, while others built entirely new castles. No doubt this was, to a great extent, escapism. They wanted to turn away from dirty factories and the prosaic figures of profit and loss, and relax in a fantasy world of chivalry – as extolled by Lord Tennyson, the Poet Laureate, in his poems about King Arthur. At the same time, there were many who studied castles seriously as a help in understanding the medieval civilisation that had produced them.

By the twentieth century the governments in several countries were coming to think that they ought to preserve ancient buildings. Their reasons were often educational and cultural, but also patriotic; these buildings were part of the national heritage, reminders of the nation's growth and traditions. Then tourism became a major industry, and they realised that ancient monuments could attract a lot of money.

So castles became valuable again. Many, it is true, were already reduced to shapeless heaps of stone, and many more were still left to decay because they were not thought important enough to justify the cost of repair. But many others, after the years of desertion and neglect, prospered again and were crowded once more with people.

Glossary

bailey — the open space enclosed by the walls of a castle

barbican — a wall extending in a loop from the curtain wall of a castle, in front of the gatehouse

barmkin — an enclosure or yard next to a tower-house, where animals were kept

battlement — the upper section of a castle wall containing open spaces used by soldiers in defending the castle

bawn — an Irish name for a yard next to a tower-house

belfry — a tall wooden tower that attackers could move up to a castle's walls during a siege; a siege tower

bombards — large guns used to attack castles during the fifteenth century

burh — an Anglo-Saxon settlement protected by an earth bank and palisade

buttery — a storeroom for ale and wine

concentric castle — a castle protected by outer walls that completely surrounded the inner wall

crenel — a gap or opening in a castle's battlements through which defenders could fire weapons or drop objects on attackers

curtain wall — a stone wall around a castle bailey

donjon — a stone building that served as the defensive center of a castle; a keep

enfilading — shooting along an enemy line from the side

escalade — to climb or scale a castle wall

four-square castle — a castle with a curtain wall that formed a rectangle and served as the back wall of the buildings it enclosed

garderobe — a small chamber built into the wall of a keep and used as a latrine

hoardings — wooden galleries extending from battlements, used to conceal and protect defenders during a siege

keep — a stone building that served as the defensive center of a castle and often housed the lord and his followers; a donjon

machicolations — battlements that projected from the castle walls and contained openings through which defenders could drop objects

mangonel — a siege engine powered by a tightly twisted piece of animal sinew, leather, or rope

merlon — an upright section of a battlement between the crenels

mining — making a tunnel that extended under a castle and that could be used to bring down the structure above it

moat — a deep trench around a castle, usually filled with water

motte — a cone-shaped mound located next to or within the bailey of an early castle

palisade — a wooden wall

plinth — a thickening at the base of a keep wall designed to prevent attackers from breaking through

portcullis — a heavy wooden grille at the entrance of a castle that could be raised and lowered

rath — a circular enclosure of earth and wood that served as a home for Irish farmers

revetment — a timber support used to strengthen a palisade

ribat — a stronghold in Muslim lands used to defend a frontier against unbelievers

ringwork — an early castle consisting of a bailey surrounded by an earth bank and a palisade

shell — a stone wall around the edge of a motte

siege castle — a tall wooden tower that attackers could move up to a castle's walls during a siege; a belfry

solar — the main sitting-room of a castle, usually with windows facing south

symmetrical castle — a castle with a design that was exactly the same on all sides

trebuchet — a siege engine that threw missiles with a sling at the end of a long arm

yett — a heavy iron grille used in front of a wooden gate

Index

*Pages shown in italic type contain
illustrations only.*

adulterine castles, 7
Alfred the Great, 6
Appleby keep (England), *11*
Arabs, 4
arrowslits, *21*
Aydon castle (England), *40*

bailey, 7, 11, 12, 30, 32
Banos de le Encina castle (Spain), *5*
barbarian invasions, 4
barbican, 25, *26, 27*
barmkin, 42
battering ram, 12
battlements, 20-21
bawn, 43
Bayeux Tapestry, 8
Beaumaris castle (Wales), *34, 35*
Behamore (Ireland), *43*
belfry, 11, 14
Bolton castle (England), *41*
bombards, 44
boulevards, 44
bow and arrow as weapon, 14, 20, 32
Bramber castle (England), 23
Brinklow, England, Norman castle at, 7
Brougham castle (England), *28*
burh, 5, 6; of Lydford, England, *6*
buttery, 37
buttresses, 18
Byzantine Empire, 4
Byzantium, 4

Caernarvon castle (Wales), *34, 35*, 39
Caerphilly castle (Wales), 32, *33*
Castel del Monte (Italy), 29, 34
Castile, Spain, 5, 17

castle, definition of, 3
castle-monastery, 17
cat, 12
chapel in castles, 39
Charles, King of the Franks
    (Charlemagne), 5
Chateau Gaillard (Normandy), 16, 32
Civil War (England), 44
Claypotts (Scotland), *42*
Colchester keep (England), *10*
concentric castles, 32, *33*, 34, 41
Conisbrough castle, 25, *26*
constable of castle, 16, 36
Constantinople, 4
Conway castle (Wales), *34, 35*
Coucy keep (France), *19*
Craigievar, *42*
crenel, *20*, 21
crossbows, 14
Crusades, influence of, on castle
    building, 16-17
curtain wall, 12, 22, 23, 30, 41

Deal castle, *45*
defense of castle, 11, 13, 14, 20-21
donjon, 10, 39. *See also* keep.
Doune castle (England), *30*
dovecotes, 38
Dover castle (England), 16, *18*, 30
drawbridge, *24*, 25, 30
dungeons in castles, 30
Dunsoghly (Ireland), *43*
Dunstanburgh castle (England), 30-31

earth-and-wood castles, 12
Edinburgh castle (Scotland), 47
Edward I (king of England), 16, 34, 39
Elphinstone (Scotland), *42*
enfilading, 20, 22

England, castles in, 12, 16, 22, 31, 42,
    44; built by Edward I, 34-35; during
    Norman period, 7-8, 10; during 13th
    century, *26-27. See also* individual
    castles.
escalade, 14
Exeter castle (England), 25

feudal system, 6, 36
Flint castle (Wales), *22, 34*
forebuilding, 11
'four-square' castles, 41, 44
Framlingham castle (England), *22, 23*, 30
France, castles in, 6, 10, *19*, 12, 22
Frederick II (Holy Roman Emperor),
    29, 34
Fulk Nerra, Count of Anjou, 10
furnishings of castle, 37-38

garderobes, 10, 38-39
gate, 23-25
gatehouse, 23-24; as keep, 30-31
Germany, castles in, 6, *9, 17*, 31
great hall of castle, 7, 10, 36-37
gunports, 44
guns, effect of, on castle-building, 44-45

Hampton Court (England), 47
Harlech castle (Wales), 30, *34, 35*
Helmsley castle (England), *27*
Henry VIII (king of England), 45
Henry the Fowler (Germany), 6
hoardings, *20*, 21
Holy Roman Empire, 5
Hundred Years' War, 44
Hurstmonceux castle (England), 44

Ireland, castles in, 43

James II (king of Scotland), 44

John (king of England), 16

keep, 18, 20, 25; circular, 19; combined
    with gatehouse, 30-31; disadvantages
    of, 30; reinforcement of, 18-19;
    shell, 11-12; square, 10-11, 19
Kells, monastery of, 9
Kenliworth castle (England), 32, 33
kitchen of castle, 37
Knights Hospitallers, 17
Knights Templars, 17

Langeais, France, keep at, 10
LaRoche Guyon castle (France), 19
lord of castle, 6, 7, 30-31, 40, 41, 46;
    life of, 10, 36-39

machicolation, 20, 21, 24
Magyars, invasion of, 6
mangonel, 12, 13
manor houses, 40
Margat (Crusader castle), 17
Marienberg castle (Germany), 17
Maxstoke castle (England), 40
merlon, 21
mining used against castle, 13-14
moat, 25
Moors, 5
motte, 8, 11
motte-and-bailey castle, 8, 10
Muiden castle (Holland), 41
'murder-holes', 24
Muslims, 4, 17; in Spain, 4-5

Netherlands, castles in, 41
Newcastle upon Tyne keep (England), 18

Orford castle, 18, 19

palisades, 7, 8, 30

pele, 42
Pembroke castle (England), 26
Penshurst Place (England), 36
penthouse, 12
Philip Augustus (king of France), 16
plinth, 19
political role of castles, 6-7, 16, 36, 46
portcullis, 25, 30

raths, 43
Ravenscraig castle (Scotland), 44-45
revetments, 7
Rhuddlan castle (Wales), 34
ribat, 17
Richard Lion Heart (king of England),
    14, 16
ringworks, 8
Rochester castle, 10, 15, 30
Roman Empire, collapse of, 4
Roman fortifications, 4
Romantic Revival, castles and, 3, 48
royal castles, 16, 29, 34, 39, 45, 46, 47

St Ulrichsburg castle (Germany), 9
sanitation in castle, 10, 38-39
scaling ladders, 14
Scot, Sir Walter, 48
Scotland, castles in, 9, 42, 44
shieldwall, 31
siege castle, 14
siege of castle, 12-14
solar, 37
Spain, 4-5; castles in, 5, 17, 41
spur, 19
stone as building material, 4, 8
Sween, Castle (Scotland), 9
symmetrical castle, 32, 34

Tantallon castle (England), 31-32
Termoli castle (Italy), 29

torre albarrana, 22
tower, 19, 22; in curtain walls, 22, 30,
    31; protecting gate, 11, 23-24
tower-houses, 42-43
Tower of London, 10, 38, 47
trebuchet, 12, 13
Trematon castle (England), 11
turrets, 20

Vikings, invasions of, 6

Wales, castles in, 16, 19, 34, 35, 39
Warkworth castle (England), 27, 47
weapons used in siege of castle, 12, 13,
    14, 20-21, 24
wells in castles, 38
Windsor castle (England), 47
wood as building material, 4, 5, 8

yett, 25

Acknowledgments

The author and publisher would like to thank the following for permission to reproduce illustrations;

front cover, p35 Cadw Welsh Historic Monuments; p1 Colin Platt *The Castle in Medieval England and Wales*, Secker and Warburg 1982; pp 8 (E.S. Armitage *Early Norman Castles of the British Isles*, 1912), 19r (Viollet-le-Duc *Military Architecture*, 1879), 40lt (T.H. Turner & J.H. Parker *Domestic Architecture in England*, 1877), 46l (John Muller *Treatise of Fortifications*, 1746) The Syndics of Cambridge University Library; p9lt Peter Harbison *Guide to the National Monuments in the Republic of Ireland*, Gill and Macmillan 1975, drawing by Brian O'Halloran; pp 9r, 32t Crown Copyright, Historic Buildings and Monuments (Scotland); pp 9lb, 32b Roger-Viollet; pp 10, 11, 22b, 26b, 36, 41l, 44 Country Life; p17t l'Institut Français d'Archéologie du Proche Orient; p17b Helga Schmidt-Glassner; pp 18r, 26t, 27, 38t, 39, 46r Historic Buildings and Monuments Commission for England; p19l © Vu du Ciel by Alain Perceval ®; p22t Cambridge University Collection, Crown Copyright Reserved; p24 © Arch. Phot. Paris/S.P.A.D.E.M; p29 The Mansell Collection; pp 30, 33, 40r, 47l, 48 Aerofilms; pp 37t (MS Add 42130 f 207), 38b (MS Ar. 157 f71v) British Library; p37b Master and Fellows of Trinity College Cambridge; p41r Rijksdienst voor de Monumentenzorg, The Netherlands; p42 Nigel Tranter *The Fortified House in Scotland*, 1962/The Syndics of Cambridge University Library; p43c,b Harold Leask *Irish Castles*, Dundalgan Press (W. Tempest) Ltd/The British Architectural Library, RIBA London; p45lt The Board of Trustees of the Royal Armouries; p45lb The British Architectural Library, RIBA London from David McGibbon and Thomas Ross *Castellated and Domestic Architecture of Scotland*, 1887; p45r Trustees of the British Museum; back cover Photographie Giraudon/Musée Condé, Chantilly.

Front cover: *Rhuddlan castle, built 1277-82 as part of Edward I's plan to take and hold North Wales (page 34). It is a concentric castle. The centre is a square inner bailey with corners guarded by two round towers and two gate-houses. The outer ring of defences is less compact and symmetrical because it has to reach the bank of the river Clwyd and cover the dock (on the right). The picture shows how the castle probably looked when it was new.*

Title page: *Caerlaverock castle, watching over one of the routes into south-west Scotland, was built about ten years after Rhuddlan. It lacks an outer ring of defences (except a good moat) but otherwise shows similar ideas of fortification: a compact, high-walled bailey with tower or gate-house at each corner. The drawing shows the castle as it is today, the original powerful design surviving despite a history of damage and repair.*

Back cover: *Castle life at its most agreeable. A scene from the calendar in a sumptuous prayer book made at the beginning of the fifteenth century for the Duke of Berry, a close relative of the King of France.*

It is August. In the countryside near the castle of Etampes some young nobles go hawking. Two ladies ride behind gentlemen, another rides by herself and the falconer—a highly skilled and valued member of the castle staff—leads the way on foot. Nearer the castle peasants are harvesting grain, and in the heat of the summer day some have taken time off to bathe in the stream.

Maps by Reg Piggott
Reconstruction drawings by Sharon Pallent,
Alan Sorell and Brian O'Halloran